GREAT
SPORTS
CARS
OF THE WORLD

GREAT
SPORTS
CARS
OF THE WORLD

CHARTWELL
BOOKS, INC.

The elegance of the Mercedes 540K Special Roadster of 1936 is virtually unsurpassable. The 8-cylinder engine produced 160 bhp, while a conservative estimate of the top speed would be 106 mph (170 kph). Five of the 25 models produced are still in existence

A Ferrari Testarossa, a
Pininfarina masterpiece of
timeless beauty. Top speed:
187.5 mph (exactly 300
kph) Above: Porsche 356/2
of 1949: and (RIGHT) the
unforgettable Horch Eagle

CONTENTS

Isotta-Fraschini engine of 1926

The last Bugatti sports-racing car before the war was the 57S (or 57SC with supercharger) with a 3.3 liter straight-eight engine; it had twin overhead cam-shafts and produced 140bhp unsupercharged and 200 bhp supercharged

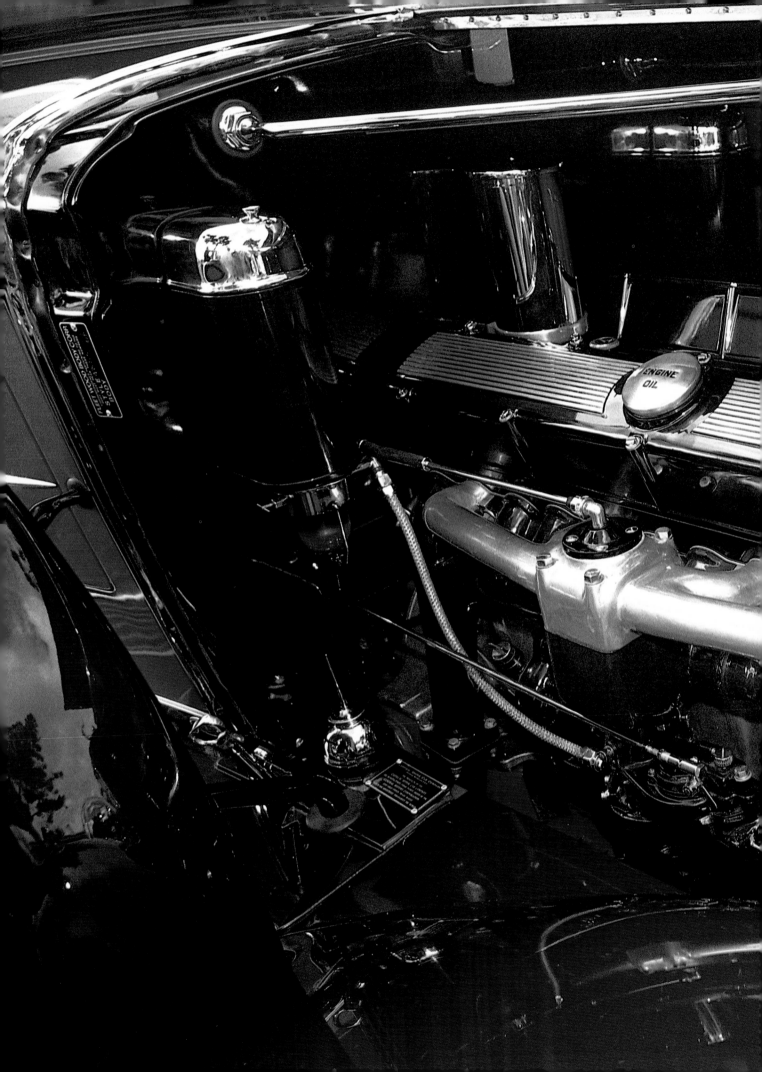

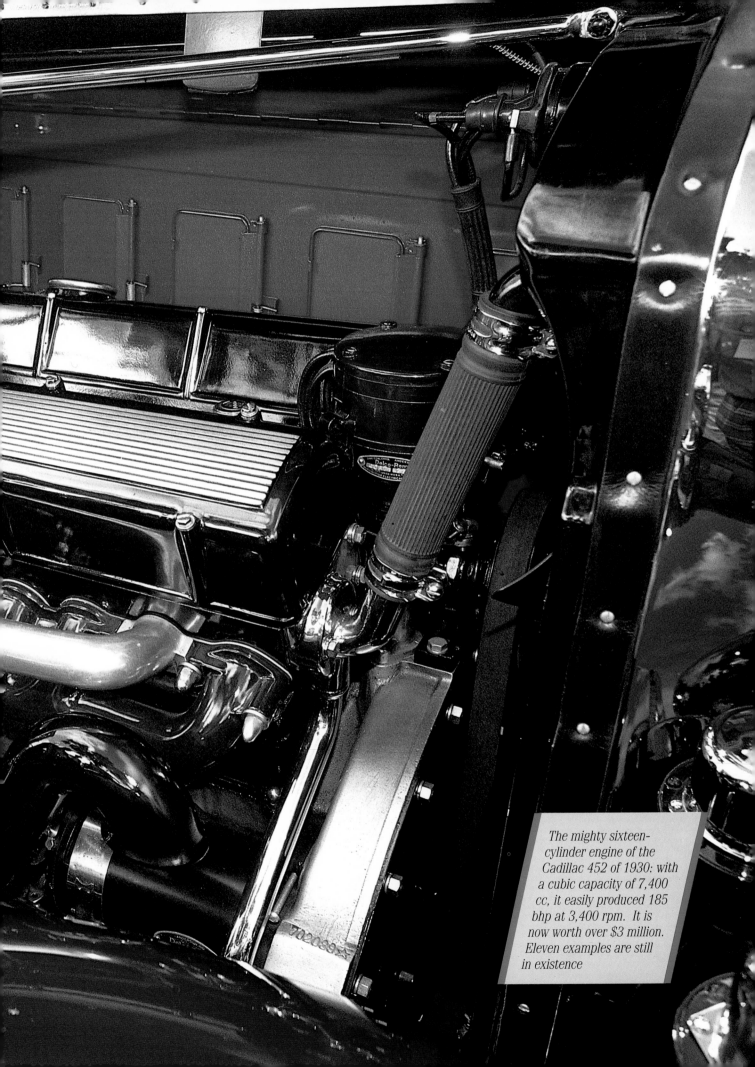

The mighty sixteen-cylinder engine of the Cadillac 452 of 1930: with a cubic capacity of 7,400 cc, it easily produced 185 bhp at 3,400 rpm. It is now worth over $3 million. Eleven examples are still in existence

Rolls-Royces were also produced in America before the Second World War. This Murphy Rolls-Royce is a particularly valuable example. It changed hands for nearly $2 million

KRUSE INTERNATIONAL
CAR CARD

Make RR Year 33
Model PhantomII Engine
Sale Number 569

DO NOT TOUCH

569

The bob-tailed Auburn Speedster was extremely popular in 1932. The company promised: "The speed of an airplane, the luxury of a yacht and the comfort of a sofa"

A FASCINATION WITH SPEED

From the start, the stars of the full throttle brigade found fame in the great races

This 9-liter Laurel sports-racing car from 1920 is unique and still takes part in Californian vintage races with all its old vigor. Output 75bhp, top speed 85 mph (135 kph)

63.25 mph (101.20 kph) average for the first Grand Prix

In the first races at the turn of the century, most of the cars were just touring cars with a few minor alterations. Gradually a few cars came to be made specially for particular races, but it was not until 1906 that racing cars began to be built in earnest. In that year the first Grand Prix in automobile history was held on a triangular course at Le Mans, each lap of which measured 64 miles (103 kilometers). The total distance of 772.5 miles imposed enormous demands on both drivers and

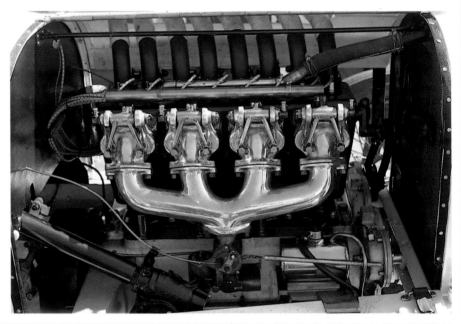

Stutz racer of 1915 (engine above). Winner of many races, but never achieved success in the Indianapolis 500. The company was in existence from 1911 to 1935

This beautifully restored Opel 5/12 Torpedo has a 1.3 liter four-cylinder monobloc engine, producing 14.5 bhp with a cubic capacity of 1800 cc. Top speed: 34 mph

The first Targa Florio: average speed 29 mph (47 kph)

mechanics. The race was won by François Szisz on a four-cylinder Renault with a capacity of 12,986 cc, at an average speed of 63 mph (101.2 kph) - seven tyre changes out on the circuit notwithstanding.

Nazarro's Fiat, with its massive 16,286 cc 4-cylinder engine, came second. It caused a certain degree of excitement: for about 13 miles (21 kilometers) Nazarro drove with his riding mechanic hanging out of the car, acting as a counterweight for a missing wheel! The spare tyres had all been used up, but the resourceful and courageous Italian managed to reach the next spare parts depot on three wheels.

Also in 1906, the immensely wealthy Sicilian Vincenzo Florio organized the first Targa Florio on his native island. The race was won by Allessandro Cagno driving an Itala at an average speed of 29.25 mph (46.82 kph). A year later, another Itala, driven by Count Scipione, won what was then the longest road race in the world, from Peking to Paris: 10,300 miles through virtually uninhabited regions, deserts and endless marshes - perilous for both men and machines.

By around 1910, sports and racing car engines were already astonishingly highly developed. The most common type of engine had four cylinders, with combustion chambers and cylinders cast together in pairs. In-line 6-cylinder engines were used for the first time in 1903 in the Dutch-made Spyker

Dr Porsche, right, wearing cap, is proud of his Austro-Daimler 1.1 liter Sascha racing car of 1914. At the wheel is Alfred Neubauer, later manager of the Mercedes racing team

The Mercedes Simplex of 1907 is considered the most important sports car before the First World War. 70 bhp at 1,280 rpm gave a top speed of almost 60 mph (95 kph), enough to win the most important speed hillclimbs in Europe. The 6-cylinder engine with an impressive capacity of 10,179 cc

Hardly any cars finished without mechanical trouble

and the British Napier. The first straight-eight engine was developed by the American Alexander Winton as early as 1903. The gigantic 22.5 liter Darracq racing engine of 1905 was the first V8 engine.

The 12-cylinder engine made its début in 1904, having been developed by the British engine-makers Craig & Dorwald for a speedboat. There were no 12-cylinder car engines until 1916, when Packard proudly introduced one to the public. Output: around 75 bhp at 2,000 rpm.

Probably the most important racing engine before the First World War was the one made by Peugeot. In April 1912 the first 4-cylinder engine with twin overhead camshafts and four valves per cylinder spluttered into life. The innovative dry sump lubrication system ensured a reliable oil supply. The new cylinder heads and the spherical combustion chambers provided greater output at high engine speeds.

This advanced engine outclassed the other successful racing engines of the time produced by Fiat, Itala, Mercedes and Opel. The small, short-stroke engine, free-revving and light in weight, produced better lap times than its excessively large and heavy long-stroke rivals.

Count Masetti wins the 1922 Targa Florio in a Mercedes. Average speed 39.375 mph (63 kph)(above). Le Mans proclamation 1906. The birth of the first Grand Prix

The 12-liter, 16-valve Opel of 1914, with Carl Jörn at the wheel, was still winning important races in 1920. The 260 bhp colossus recorded a speed of 141.25 mph (226 kph) on Fanî beach! It won a total of 200 races

By 1932, Indianapolis was already one of the fastest, most dangerous race tracks in the world. Milt Jones died because of a burst tyre

During the hard times of the
Great Depression the most
luxurious sports cars were built
in America. The incomparably
elegant Duesenberg Speedsters
created a sensation with their
astonishing performance

THE GLITZ AND GLAMOUR OF THE 1930S

America's classic sports cars - precious gems of automobile history

At the beginning of the 1930s there were only 5,200 people living in Auburn. For American sports car enthusiasts, however, this small town, rather than the car-manufacturing centre of Detroit with its population of more than a million, was the centre of the universe. There were good reasons for this. Three sports car firms had their works here: Duesenberg, Auburn and Cord. Depending on the state of the order book, the same factory workers assembled an Auburn, a Cord or a Duesenberg. There was, however, a small difference in the selling price:

at around $15,000 the cheapest Duesenberg was ten times as expensive as an Auburn or a Cord.

Throughout their lives, the brothers Fred Samuel and August Samuel Duesenberg, who came from Lippe in Westphalia, Germany, were interested more in motor racing than in commercial matters. Fred S. Duesenberg died of pneumonia in 1932. Even before then, his brother August had gradually had to surrender his shares in the company to the stock market speculator Errett Lobban Cord. By 1932, Auburn, Cord and Duesenberg

This high-performance
Cord L29 of 1929, with
brougham bodywork, was
a brilliant front-wheel
drive design. Lycoming
FDA straight-eight engine;
4,900 cc capacity giving
125 bhp at 3,600 rpm

Ab Jenkins and his Duesenberg SJ supercharged monster

were finally under Cord's exclusive ownership, as was the Lycoming engine plant.

August S. Duesenberg remained with Cord as chief designer. On Cord's instructions, Duesenberg developed a race-tested supercharged engine for the Auburns and Cords. Nobody overtook Duesenberg's SJ supercharged Speedster. In the 1930s, a roadster with a 90 bhp engine was considered high-powered, but even the least powerful Duesenberg J Speedster treated its owner to a mighty 265 bhp. In 1932, the robust straight-eight engine was also fitted with a Cummins centrifugal supercharger. This meant that an incredible 320 bhp was available for overtaking. In 1935, racing driver Ab Jenkins and designer August S. Duesenberg gave the 6.8 liter engine a further power boost to 390 bhp, and at Bonneville on the Great Salt Lake in Utah they set a new world 24-hour record with an average speed of exactly 139.9 mph (223.96 kph).

Duesenberg drivers did not talk a lot about money - they had enough of it. Hollywood's darlings - notably Greta Garbo and members of the smart set such as Clark Gable and Gary Cooper - trusted in their own charm and in that of their highly polished Speedsters. Anybody who drove a Duesenberg was, in that respect at least, in a very special class.

Duesenberg cars were made for only 17 years. The English motor historian

The fastest sports car of the 1930s was undoubtedly this 390 bhp Duesenberg SJ Speedster. Ab Jenkins set a 24-hour world record in it with an average speed of 150 mph (240 kph)

Duesenbergs: ten times the price of the average sports car

Michael Sedgwick refers to 1,250 examples built between 1920 and 1937. The American Duesenberg expert Fred Roe lists a total of 2,614 cars. Nobody can prove exactly how many Duesenbergs were actually built. The fame of this luxury car is out of all proportion to the production figures.

Five hundred and eighty-eight of the famous straight-eight engines were produced at Lycoming. Duesenberg's first roadgoing sports car was the Model A, which was powered by a 4.25 liter straight-eight engine with a single overhead camshaft. This was the first American sports car to be equipped with hydraulic brakes. Between 1920 and 1926, 498 examples were delivered. Its successor, the Model J, with its twin-camshaft 6.9 liter engine with or without supercharger, consolidated the marque's reputation as the most powerful car in America, if not the whole world.

Not many cars were actually fitted with the supercharged engine: 36 engines of between 320 and 395 bhp were supplied by Lycoming. Even with a 320 bhp engine, an SJ speedster can accelerate from a standing start to 103 mph (165 kph) in just 17 seconds. Since the car weighs over two and a half tons, this acceleration shows how much torque is produced by the engine. There are only three speeds: First can be used all the way from a standstill to about 55 mph (90 kph). Second takes the car up to about 90 mph (150 kph) and in third a top speed of 133 mph

Nobody could buy a Duesenberg off the peg. Each car had its own unique body style and interior trim. This Rollston convertible is valued at over $3 million

Chrome-plated wire wheel of a Duesenberg (LEFT). The American classics of the 1930s are impressively large: this Murphy Lincoln, seen in the streets of Auburn, is almost 20 ft (6 m) long and over 5 ft (1.6 m) high

The 16-cylinder Marmon: one of the first V16s in history

(214 kph) can be reached (source: Road & Track).

In comparison with some of the largest European and American engines, the 6.9 liters of the Duesenberg engine was relatively modest; nevertheless, it was a consummate high-performance power unit, suitable for use in racing cars. At that time, for example, Renault was equipping its 45 with a 9.1 liter engine, while the V12 Hispano Suiza had a cubic capacity of 9.4 liters. The 16-cylinder Marmon and Cadillac engines of 8 and 7.4 liters produced 200 and 160 bhp respectively.

From 1934, the Cord group's chief designer was Gordon Buehrig, who had previously worked for General Motors. He had left GM because the company's management had not liked his revolutionary front-wheel drive car. At Cord, however, the front-wheel drive system was seen as a new opportunity. Gordon Buehrig's front-wheel drive Cord 810/812 was both technically and stylistically twenty years ahead of its time. However, the collapse of the Auburn-Cord-Duesenberg automobile company in the autumn of 1937 did not come out of the blue. In August 1986, Gordon Buehrig recalled: "As early as the mid-1930s, we were building the Duesenberg chassis only to firm orders. Lycoming supplied the engines, and the bodies were made by outside companies. The coachbuilders earned a great deal of money, while we made virtually nothing. Before the Great

The great rivals of the imposing Duesenbergs, Cadillacs and Marmons were the 1930 V12 Lincoln (radiator mascot on the left), the Pierce Arrows and the Packards. In the mid-1930s, maximum engine performance was less sought after than optimum comfort

The unbelievably quiet 16-cylinder Marmon engine can hardly be heard when it is idling. The 8-liter engine produces 200 bhp at 3,200 rpm with ease (pictures left and below)

**Money didn't enter
the equation with a
Lincoln V12 roadster**

Crash on the stock exchange, the
Auburns sold very well. In 1934, only
4,800 cars were sold, compared with
the peak year of 1931 when more than
30,000 were sold. From the technical
point of view, only the Cord 810 was a
new car with a future. We saw that
car as a small Duesenberg. I started
work on it in 1934; by January 1936,
the prototype was on display at the
New York Motor Show." The initially
unsatisfactory model went into series
production without adequate testing,
very much to the company's detriment,
as it later transpired. Its improved
successor did little to change matters.
"In 1937, the 812 went into production, with a range of power units
producing up to 195 bhp. Handling
was first class, and most of the
problems with engines overheating and
gears jumping out had been eliminated.
However, the company's reputation
was ruined, because those who had
bought the car the year before felt they
had been used as test drivers. Fifty
years on, I can say that the collapse of
the company could have been
avoided."

The plant of the former Cord empire
passed into the hands of Hupmobile.
Cars with Cord bodywork and a six-
cylinder Graham engine were built
there until 1941. However, success
remained elusive. Today, Auburn
Speedster replicas with Chevrolet
engines can be seen on American
roads, and an extremely ugly, flashy
dreamboat-style Duesenberg was

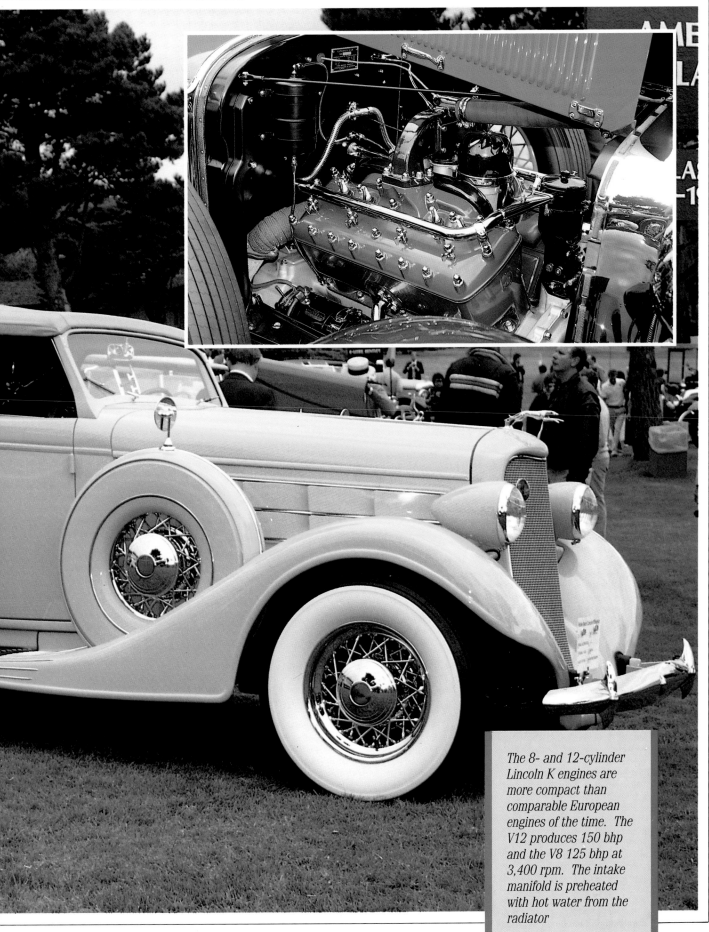

The 8- and 12-cylinder Lincoln K engines are more compact than comparable European engines of the time. The V12 produces 150 bhp and the V8 125 bhp at 3,400 rpm. The intake manifold is preheated with hot water from the radiator

**Duesenberg racing
cars won the French
GP and Indy 500**

introduced as a prototype in the mid-1970s. Fortunately, the nephew of the company's founder quickly realized that there is more to making cars than a famous name.

Car lovers will seldom set eyes on an original Duesenberg with a straight-eight engine in Europe. At the Duesenberg Museum in the former Cord factory in Auburn, they reckon there are only about ten such Duesenbergs in Europe. About 300 straight-eight Duesenbergs remain in roadworthy condition. Considering that total production was only 588 cars at most, no other company to date has produced such a long-lived product.

At the beginning of 1988, the price at auction for a restored Duesenberg was about $1 million. The Harrah Automobile Museum in Reno, Nevada makes spare parts to order. Just to buy a crankshaft will set you back about $40,000. As in the 1930s, a Duesenberg still epitomizes the unique attractions of the luxury sports car.

Duesenberg racing cars dominated the big American races for years. Customers wanted more comfort; however, this cross between a racing car and a sports coupé remained an experiment. (INSET) *The beautiful straight-eight engine standard 1931 production model*

Perfection in every detail. The classics of the 1930s are rightly considered the most valuable cars in history. A duplex (a large house for two families) could be had for less in America than a Cadillac or a Duesenberg. The present-day value of these cars is between $2 million and $7.5 million

HIGH-SPEED ELEGANCE

The bewitching Europeans with their sweeping lines

The perfectly shaped Mercedes 540K was one of the few luxury roadsters that looked extremely elegant in standard form. As a result, few 540Ks were fitted with special bodywork

Hispano-Suiza J12 coupé with 9,425 cc cubic capacity and 220 bhp. Swiss designer Marc Birkigt developed the most powerful V12 engines of the 1930s. Only the seriously rich could afford to drive this marque

Rudi Caracciola and the legendary 'white elephants'

For sports car enthusiasts of the 1930s, Rudolf Caracciola and his 'white elephant' - so called because the car was white and the huge supercharger was known as an 'elephant blower' - were the perfect racing partnership. The Mercedes SS was a monster of a sports car. Its 7-liter, in-line six-cylinder engine with a shrilly howling Roots supercharger both sounded and looked perfectly capable of producing 300 bhp and a top speed of over 125 mph (200 kph) in racing trim. In his gripping book 'Men, Women and Motoring', Alfred Neubauer, the Mercedes racing team chief, depicts the unfolding of the 1928 German Grand Prix at the Nürburgring more vividly than any other eyewitness:

"The supercharger of Rudi Caracciola's SS is howling along merrily out in front. And behind him, a long way ahead of the others, the 'white elephants' driven by Merz and Werner. Where are they, all the famous French and Italian aces? Tenth lap: Caracciola comes into the pits. The right-hand rear tyre is torn to shreds. Tyre change. Two precious minutes trickle away. Rudi gulps down a glass of water. It's amazing how this puny-looking young man handles the car. Eleventh lap: Caracciola is trying to make up the lost time. He roars past the stands at 125 mph (200 kph) - and this in a car that I wouldn't like to drive today at 50 (80 kph). Twelfth lap: What's the matter? Has Rudi bitten off

The Horch 853A cabriolet of 1937 with a special Fleetwood body. The straight-eight engine is fitted with twin overhead camshafts (RIGHT: the Horch eagle)

A Bentley, four times winner at Le Mans in the 1920s, epitome of the classic English sports car. This is a shortened and lowered 8 liter

Drivers of the not overly sporty 8-cylinder Horch were spoilt by its reliability. From 1920, Paul Daimler, chief designer at Horch, produced technically superb and luxuriously comfortable cars

In 1931 there were 100 8-liter Bentleys. 78 are still around

Bentley sports cars (RIGHT AND BELOW) *won several victories at Le Mans and Brooklands. The 7,893 cc 6-cylinder engine* (CENTRE) *produced 200 bhp. The Belgian Minerva car enjoyed a high reputation. The sleeve-valve straight-six AF engine displays technical perfection* (BOTTOM)

more than he can chew? He stops at the pits, sitting wearily in his seat. I look into his ashen face: 'I can't go on,' he mumbles. Then he slumps further back in his seat.... Caracciola has blisters on his feet. The heat of the engine has been transmitted to the accelerator pedal, making it almost red-hot. We work like a boxer's seconds... then Rudi drops back into the seat...." Together with the old campaigner Harald Merz, Rudolf Caracciola won the German Grand Prix. By the end, Merz had a dislocated shoulder, while Caracciola had heatstroke and burnt feet. It was Caracciola's second Grand Prix victory. In 1926, while still a private entrant, he had won in pouring rain at the Avus, since when his colleagues had called him the 'rainmaster'. The public simply adored Rudi.

Very few drivers drove the Mercedes SS on the limit. Its two massive rigid axles meant that its handling was tricky to say the least.

Around 1930, there were also some sports-racing cars from England that could only be tamed by the best of the full-throttle brigade. These were the incomparable green Bentleys - high, long and pretty heavy, perhaps the most typical representatives of the vintage era. The largest, the 8 liter, tipped the scales at up to 2.6 tons, and yet in the 1920s Bentleys won the Le Mans 24 hour race five times. Walter Owen Bentley had worked in aero-engine design during the First World

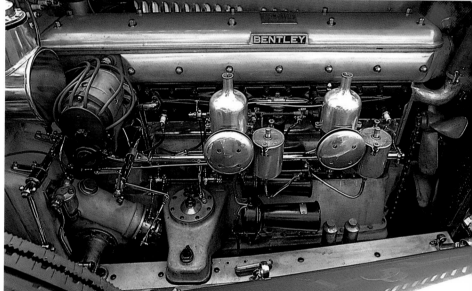

The Du Pont was a luxury car. 537 were sold between 1920 and 1932. The Merrimac G is powered by an 8-cylinder 12K Continental engine. Value: $1.25 million

The Bentley Boys beat all comers

In 1919, the Italian company Isotta Fraschini became one of the first European manufacturers to equip its cars with brakes on all four wheels. Star of the silent films Rudolph Valentino ran three Isottas at the same time

war and was honored by King George V for his work. His sports cars turned out to be suitably powerful and long-lived - a five-year chassis guarantee was quite unique in 1930.

Bentley's almost obsessive attitude to motor sport is reflected in the extremely ambitious specification of his 3-liter 4-cylinder engine. The crankshaft had five main bearings. It was unusual at that time for what was fundamentally a fast touring machine to have four valves per cylinder. Aluminium pistons and a pressurized lubrication system with a separate sump meant that high engine speeds could be sustained. Two sparking-plugs per cylinder with twin synchronized magnetos assisted the combustion process. In addition to the 3-liter engine producing as standard 72 bhp at 3,500 rpm, W.O. Bentley developed a 4.5-liter engine whose output was later boosted with a supercharger from 115 bhp through 182 bhp to a maximum of 250 bhp, depending on the occasion. It was this engine (in unsupercharged form) that powered the car driven by the Bentley team of Rubin and Barnato to victory in the 1928 Le Mans race, despite stiff competition from the American Stutz and Chrysler teams. Their average speed was 69.5 mph (111.23 kph).

The most astonishing thing about the 4.5-liter supercharged Bentley was its pulling power in top gear. Drivers averse to shifting gear could accelerate from 12 mph (20 kph) to maximum speed without shifting down. The Bentley company suffered from a

A dream car of the pre-war years. The last Bugatti coupés built before 1940 were the 57S and 57SC Atlantic and Atlanta (shown here). 3.3 liter 8-cylinder engine; 134 mph (215 kph)

Rien ne l'arrête
ni les températures extrêmes
ni les rampes les plus fortes
ni les mauvais chemins

c'est une
BERLIET

JOSEPH CHARLES PARIS

RENAULT

Gran Premio D'Europa l'e II° "FIAT"

FIAT

LES LORRAINES

SOCIÉTÉ LORRAINE
DES ANCIENS ÉTABLISSEMENTS
DE DIETRICH & Cie DE LUNÉVILLE

NEU PIRELLI

Posters from the early days of automobile history show that sportiness was generally in demand. Brilliant technical achievements and high speeds were strong selling points

With a wheelbase of almost 13 feet (4 meters), the Isotta Fraschinis are some of the longest cars ever built. A coupé de ville weighed almost 3 tons. These cars were a good ten times more expensive than the most expensive Ford in the 1930s

The impressive smoothness of the Isotta 8-cylinder engine is shown here. Even with the fan whirring, a sharp photograph can still be taken at 1/30th sec. exposure

Frenchman Gabriel Voisin made more than 10,000 fighter aircraft before producing cars with sleeve-valve engines, including a twelve-cylinder

In 1938, Bugatti fell into financial difficulties. The Type 57, here with bodywork by Gangloff of Colmar, failed to halt the company's decline. It had a 3.3 liter engine, and hydraulic brakes on all four wheels

At the beginning of the 1930s, no more money was being earned with lavish designs such as this 16-valve Sizaire Fräres engine dating from 1924

Harry A. Miller was known both as a lady's man and a devotee of powerful engines. Miller-engined racing cars were frequent winners at Indianapolis

His girlfriend was the no less celebrated Lilian Harvey (RIGHT) who drove Mercedes 540K sports cars

Of a more down-to-earth disposition, the uncrowned king of the mountains, Luis Trenker, put his faith in 1932 in his sturdy 1.2 liter Opel - at that time a true people's car (LEFT)

The front-wheel drive Cord L29 impresses by its sheer size. The driver gazes out over a hood almost 10 feet (3 meters) in length

The Cadillac 6-liter of 1931 was equipped with a suction fuel pump. Output 135 hp at 3,400 rpm

The dainty Elly Beinhorn left not only the best flying aces trailing in her slipstream. In 1932, she drove her mighty Mercedes SS through Berlin with equal aplomb

The internationally famous tenor Richard Tauber drove a Mercedes 630 Tourer. Man and machine in concert

Widespread bankruptcies in the automobile sector

chronic shortage of funds, but through energetic sponsorship the firm acquired the means to produce new, even more daring designs. The diamond million-aire Woolf Barnato, one of the richest men in England, and the no less wealthy Dorothy Paget helped out with large injections of cash and took an active part in the company's racing activities. The legendary reputation of Bentley sports cars was further strengthened by the new six-cylinder Speed Six engine, with a capacity of 6.5 liters. The 'Bentley Boys' - Birkin, Barnato, Kidston and Rubin - drove it to victory in the Double-Twelve and 500 Miles races at the Brooklands high speed racing circuit, and in the Le Mans 24-hour race. During these years, the Bentleys reduced many a promising rival to the ranks of the also-rans. By the end of 1930, 182 Speed Sixes, and 363 Standard Sixes for the discerning 'ordinary driver', had been built.

The time was now ripe for an even more powerful engine. The answer to the great Continental luxury cars produced by Mercedes, Hispano Suiza and others, and to the big Rolls-Royce Phantom II, was the 8 liter Bentley. The mighty 7,982 cc, 6-cylinder engine with dual ignition produced 220 bhp. Perhaps the aesthete Ettore Bugatti's alleged description of the Bentley racers as "the fastest trucks in the world" applies even more to this model. Only 100 were sold, but by then W.O. Bentley's celebrated sports car

Aviation engineers recognized the value of streamlining as a means of improving performance. However, commercial success with motor vehicles was limited. Aerodynamic shapes appealed only to a few advanced thinkers

The King of Iraq had himself driven through Baghdad in 1935 in this Mercedes 500K roadster

Paul Jaray is considered the father of streamlining. This Mercedes 540 (ABOVE) was developed in 1938 for testing Dunlop tyres. Jaray's most famous design is the rear-engined Tatra

This rare contemporary photograph shows André Dubonnet's first streamlined car of 1936. A vertical fin towers above the rear engine. The front wheel spats are fixed to the wheel hubs and move with the wheels to allow cornering. An attractive design in terms of aerodynamics, but of course nobody wanted to buy it

The war casts its dark shadow

company was teetering on the brink of ruin. The company went into liquidation in 1931 and was bought by Rolls-Royce for £125,265. W.O. Bentley retired from the limelight for a few years, re-emerging in 1935 as chief designer for Lagonda. Under Rolls-Royce's management, the fiery Bentley became a refined fast touring car, known as "the silent sports car".

The collapse of Bentley as an independent sports car company was not an isolated case in the early 1930s. Wall Street's "Black Friday", 24 October 1929, turned a lot of sports car enthusiasts into subway users. The mint in New York had to stamp 100 million new five-cent pieces because there were not enough in circulation for the automatic ticket machines. Between 1929 and 1934, 57 car manufacturers went bankrupt.

A three-day rally in the Harz mountains in Germany in 1933. Motor sport as preparation for war

*A Bentley tool set, supplied as standard
(LEFT). A rare Bugatti Type 49 Profile
Coupé of 1932. A hint of streamlining*

In 1931 a record ten hour
journey was made. The
Alfa 2-seater had no
competitors. In 1933, 500
kilometers were still
travelled without a break

THE POST-WAR REVIVAL

*Enthusiasm for sports cars
survived the war*

The legendary Alfa Romeo 8C won the Mille Miglia in 1931 and 4 Le Mans races in the 30s. The super-charged 8-cylinder engine was used in various sizes right up to the war in sports and racing cars

This flamboyant 135M Delahaye was bodied by Figoni and Falaschi in 1948 (LEFT). In 1954, the arms manufacturer Hotchkiss took over the company, which had been in existence since 1895, thus bringing to a close a glorious chapter in the history of French luxury sports cars

The most beautiful French sports cars were those produced by Bugatti and Delahaye. Shown here is the Chapron 145 coupé (FOREGROUND). The Delahaye hubcap epitomizes these cars' inimitable elegance (RIGHT)

In comparison with those in many English and German sports cars of the immediate post-war period, the French Delahaye and Talbot engines were considered extremely sporty. The three thirsty twin-choke caburetors shown here lend support to this view. Delahaye was the first European car maker to fit detachable cylinder heads. 3.5 liters, 152 bhp at 5,600 rpm

The most famous French coachbuilders gave the Delahaye sports cars bodies with emphatic curves. The price asked by Chapron for the 145 coupé would have bought 13 Citroën mid-range cars

Two of the most
important sports cars of
the post-war period were
the Porsche 356/10
(ABOVE) and the Mercedes
300 SL, with the famous
gull-wing doors. Race
victories were more
important than high sales
figures in furthering the
reputation of the German
industry. RIGHT, the
beautiful Mercedes 220 A
cabriolet of 1952

Britain against the rest of the world: the Aston Martin DB4

Just weeks after the end of the Second World War, sports cars were again rolling off the production lines of hastily patched-up factories. Nobody doubted that motor sport would make a glorious comeback. Buyers would soon return, the delight in their regained freedom sharpening their appetite for driving fast cars.

Among British cars, the MG TC, based on the 1939 TB, sold well. In 1947, Aston Martin, Jaguar and Lagonda sold 1,287 high-priced sports and luxury cars. Total production at Aston Martin today is about 200 units, but in those days the new Aston Martin boss David Brown managed to sell 1,375 DB2s to the company's still wealthy clientele.

The situation of luxury sports car manufacturers in France was very different. The state favoured small cars. Sports cars with large engines were declared a luxury and subjected to draconian rates of tax. The demise of the uniquely elegant Delahayes and Bugattis was hastened if not actually directly caused by these punitive tax laws. On the other hand, Amédée Gordini's Simca sports and racing cars sold without any difficulty, proving beyond doubt that a market for sports cars still existed. Italian sports car companies such as Ferrari (with their Barchettas, victorious for the first time in 1949), Maserati and Alfa Romeo captured the French market. In 1948, the new 2-liter, 12-cylinder Ferrari 166 won the Mille Miglia and Targa Florio.

The rapid Aston Martin DB4 Gran Turismo with up to 325 bhp was in production between 1958 and 1962. The 3.7-liter, 6-cylinder car offered tough competition for Ferrari, Lancia and Maserati. The engine was designed by Tadek Marek, a Pole who had fled to England via Casablanca during the war

Rapid recovery after the war

In 1949, the 166 (the number denoted the cubic capacity of each cylinder) won the first post-war Le Mans 24-hour race from the larger-engined Talbot and Delahaye. The car could also be used without any difficulty at all on ordinary roads as a perfectly normal sports car.

In 1952, Colin Chapman's Lotus Engineering Company made its debut as a sports and racing car manufacturer. The mechanical engineering student set up the company with start-up capital of £25 borrowed from his girlfriend Hazel. The famous Super Seven, in which racing drivers such as Graham Hill and Patrick Depailler successfully began their careers, is still being made today by Caterham.

The company founded in 1948 by Professor Ferdinand Porsche grew from being the underdog met with a pitying smile, to become perhaps the leading sports car manufacturer in the world. Porsche's ideas were similar to those embodied by Colin Chapman's Lotus: lightweight construction, outstanding aerodynamics and small, robust engines. Porsche's first overall victory in a race in the world sports car championship was achieved on 31 May 1956 in the Targa Florio. Chapman's Lotus won its first Grand Prix four years later, when Stirling Moss was the victor at Monaco.

The spartan dashboard of the Lotus Super Seven. The second Corvette prototype, produced in 1952 (FAR RIGHT)

Alfa Romeo 1900 of 1955 with Zagato body. Alfa Romeo, Lancia and Porsche scored many victories over larger racers, with their sophisticated technology and better handling

NSU Wankel Spider of 1963. Felix Wankel's experiments with rotary-piston engines started as early as the 1920s. In 1951, a contract for their manufacture was signed with NSU. In its racing version, the 500 cc rotary-piston engine produced 110 bhp

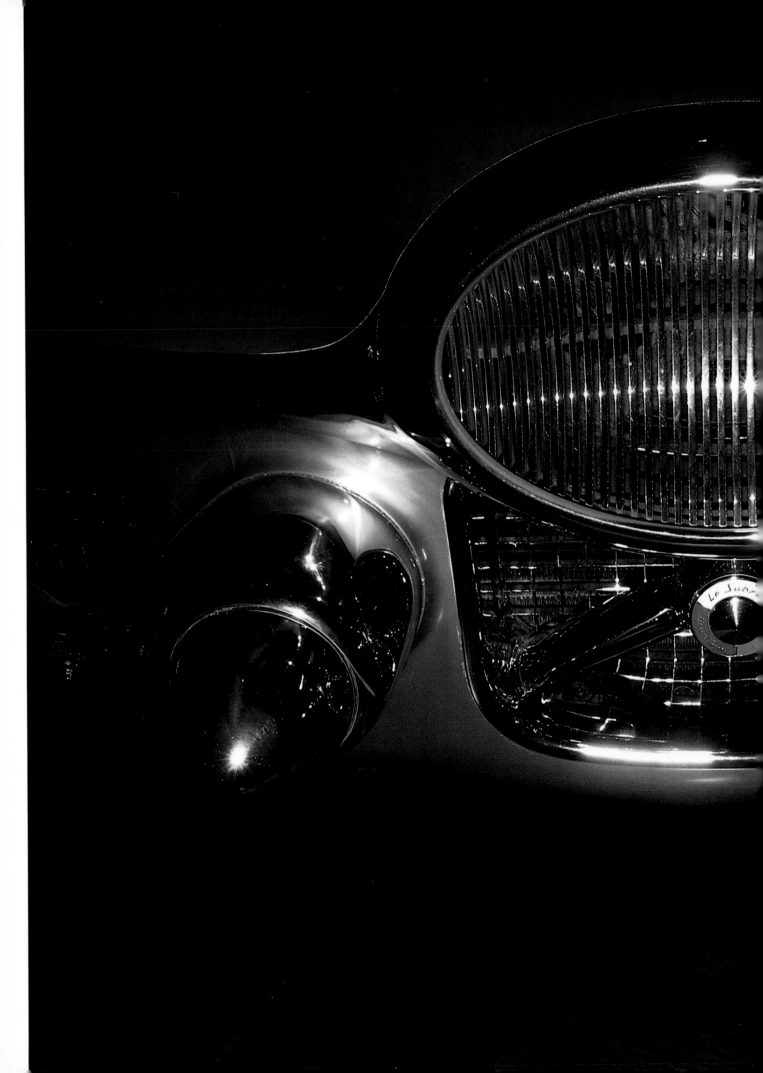

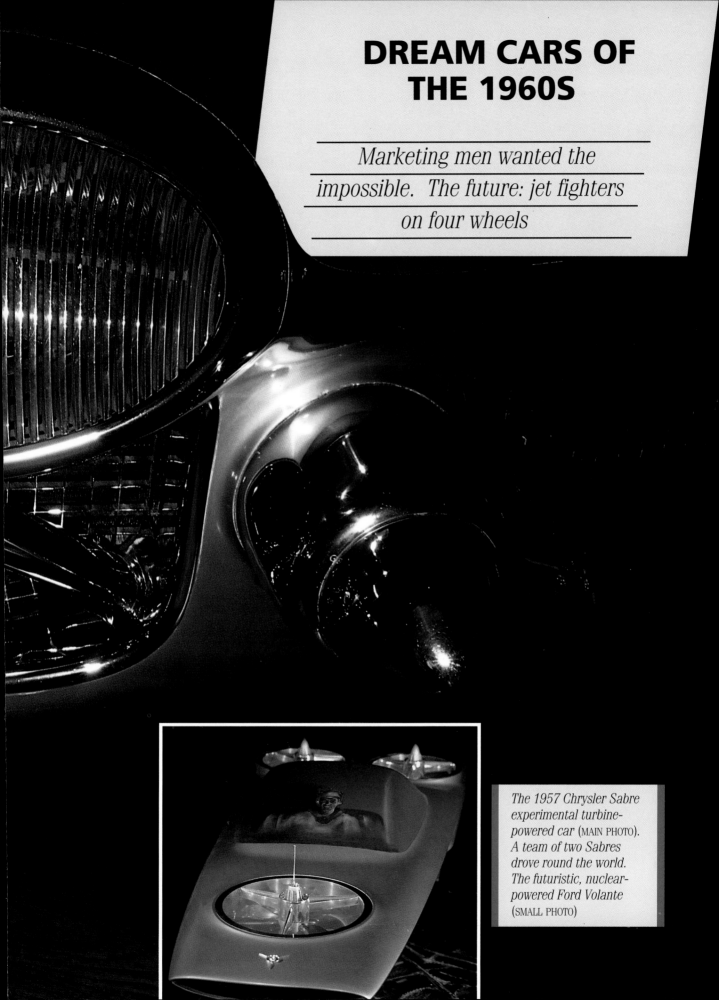

DREAM CARS OF THE 1960S

Marketing men wanted the impossible. The future: jet fighters on four wheels

The 1957 Chrysler Sabre experimental turbine-powered car (MAIN PHOTO). A team of two Sabres drove round the world. The futuristic, nuclear-powered Ford Volante (SMALL PHOTO)

1960–70

Gas turbines set new records. Europe was in on the action

The 1960s saw an economic boom in America greater than anything experienced for a long time. Only the most die-hard pessimists saw the future as anything other than prosperous. The bosses in Detroit drew on their massive resources to produce cars with fantastic styling, lavish power and maximum comfort. For a reasonable $2,160, buyers could have the 250 bhp Chevrolet Impala Sport. Its occupants sat in almost

78

General Motors' Firebird XP-21 was considered the most sensational automobile ever in 1954. The Fiat Turbine (BELOW) impressed the experts with its soaring tailfins, similar to those of the Cadillac Eldorado Biarritz (LEFT). Renault's Etoile filante on the banking at Monthlery (FAR LEFT). It broke world records in 1955 at an average speed of 193.75 mph (310 kph)

The Firebird 3 (LEFT) startled the competition with its audacious dome-shaped roof and a turbine engine of 280 bhp. Stylistically a high point of the dream car era of the 1960s

79

Full tilt down a blind alley. American dream cars of 1960

Fortunately, the Chrysler Turboflite remained a stylist's dream

unlimited comfort and there was ample room for six people on the car's plush bench seats, which cosseted young and old alike. And there was also plenty of scope for playing games: just press a button on the mother-of-pearl coloured dashboard and the roof would slide open or shut. Another gentle touch on the button controlling seat adjustment, and Momma's darling would slide, willingly or otherwise, into the reclining position. The new sports coupés were a big hit with teenagers. The enormously wide vehicles became known as dreamboats: undoubtedly they could be put to good use at certain delicate moments...

The Ford copywriters used the slogan "For the buy of your life" to promote the company's Mercury car. When General Motors' Biarritz was first unveiled, its tail-fins more than 20 inches (53 centimeters) high left journalists speechless. This was a new record even for the dreamboat era.

The dream cars conceived in the design studios attracted even more attention. General Motors' gas turbine-driven sports-racing cars made the front pages of the major newspapers. Ford countered with a nuclear-powered fantasy that was supposedly to go into series production by the late 1960s. Chrysler fitted its softly sprung Saratoga coupé with a 400 bhp 8-cylinder engine and had a turbine-powered Comet Sportster driven round the world. A car without wheels that travelled on a cushion of

The Chrysler Dart - abandoned at the last minute

Ford's six-wheeler hit the headlines

Even Cadillac dabbled with sports cars. The Cyclone experimental car, with its risqué front end, aroused the wrath of women's associations. When overtaking, the red headlights blinked

81

The Corvette accelerates out of sight: from prototype to supercar

air like a hovercraft terrified New Yorkers with its din.

The two automobile giants Ford and General Motors also produced serious sports cars. The Ford Thunderbird and the Chevrolet Corvette served as the bases for admirable special designs that outperformed European sports cars such as the Mercedes 300 SL or an Aston Martin. The Corvette SS won the GT long-distance world championship on several occasions. Carol Shelby's Cobra, based on the British AC Ace, was rightly considered the fastest accelerating GT sports car of the time, and for several years successive Ford GT 40 prototypes gave the Europeans no chance of outright victory, even in the Le Mans 24-hour race.

The Chevrolet Corvette SS and the Chevrolet Stingray have the distinction of being the first sports cars to make successful use of plastics in the bodywork. To date, more than 4 million Corvettes have been produced with bodies of laminated fibreglass and polyester resin. The dream cars of the 1960s were more than mere eyecatchers conceived by the publicity men.

1960 Chevrolet Stingray sports car, LEFT) competitive with Ferraris, but only one was ever built

Not even this beautiful Chevrolet prototype (MAIN PICTURE) went into series production (1963 Monza GT Coupé). Unlike their competitors, the Chevrolet experimental prototypes were always capable of being driven

This Pininfarina experimental car attracted a great deal of attention in Europe. The do-it-yourself magazine "Hobby" wrote: "This is how cars of the future will look." They were wrong

Chevrolet Corvette SS experimental sports-racing car (BELOW). A winner in its open-top version, known as the Astrovette (LEFT). Very similar to the 1985 Corvette

An official General Motors works team took part in the 1956 Sebring 12-hour race. Although the Corvette SS (LEFT) performed superbly, its racing program was halted afterwards

The famous no. 4: Karl
Kling's victorious 300 SL
of 1952. The car that
defeated the Ferraris in
the most important road
races of the post-war
period earned a place in
racing history

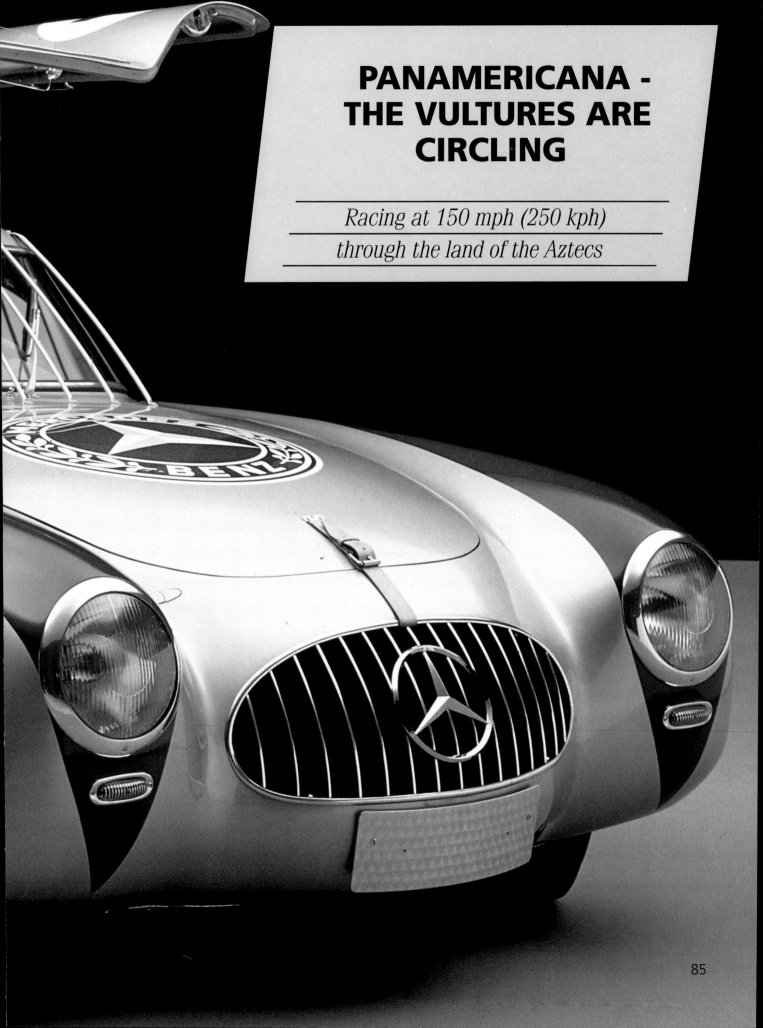

PANAMERICANA - THE VULTURES ARE CIRCLING

Racing at 150 mph (250 kph)

through the land of the Aztecs

The Ferrari 12-cylinder engines with cubic capacities between 4.1 and 4.9 liters were used in both Grand Prix and Indianapolis cars

The Lancia Aurelia with a 2-liter supercharged engine did well to come fourth in the 1952 Carrera Panamerican

At the end of the 1952 season, the Mercedes 300 SL drivers were scheduled to compete in the third Carrera Panamericana (Panamerican Road Race) in Mexico.

Their rivals were the top international racing drivers. Ferrari's team consisted of the best Grand Prix drivers in the world at the time: Ascari, Farina, Villoresi, Chinetti, Bracco and others. Umberto Maglioli drove the fastest 2-liter Lancia Aurelia with

supercharger, and Jean Behra and Robert Manzon put their faith in a 2.3 liter Gordini. Behra wanted to go solo, without the assistance of a co-driver, a risk that nobody had ever taken before. Mercedes had a good team, including the experienced long-distance racing drivers Hermann Lang and Karl Kling, as well as the talented young American John Fitch. The journalist Günther Molter, later the chief press officer at Daimler-Benz for many years,

The last Panamericana was won in 1954 by three Ferrari 375 Pluses. The picture shows Maglioli's winning car. Mercedes did not enter a team

87

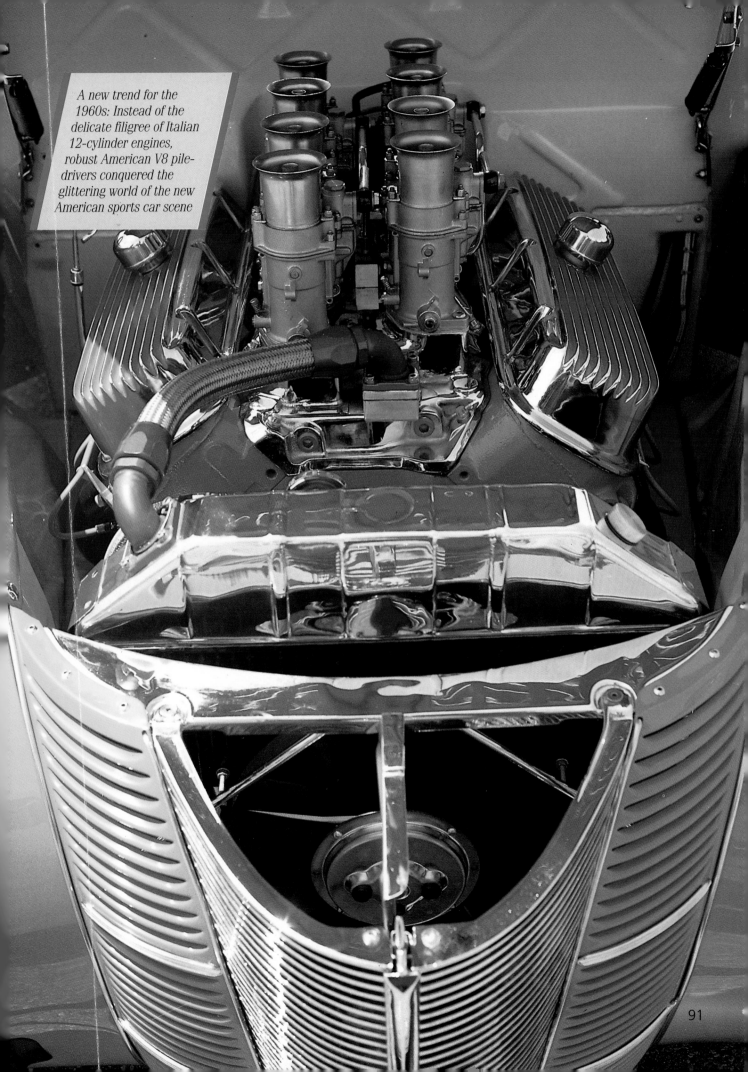

A new trend for the 1960s: Instead of the delicate filigree of Italian 12-cylinder engines, robust American V8 pile-drivers conquered the glittering world of the new American sports car scene

Introduced in 1962, the AC Cobra is still enthused over by sports car fans 30 years later; this is a German version, known as the Stallion

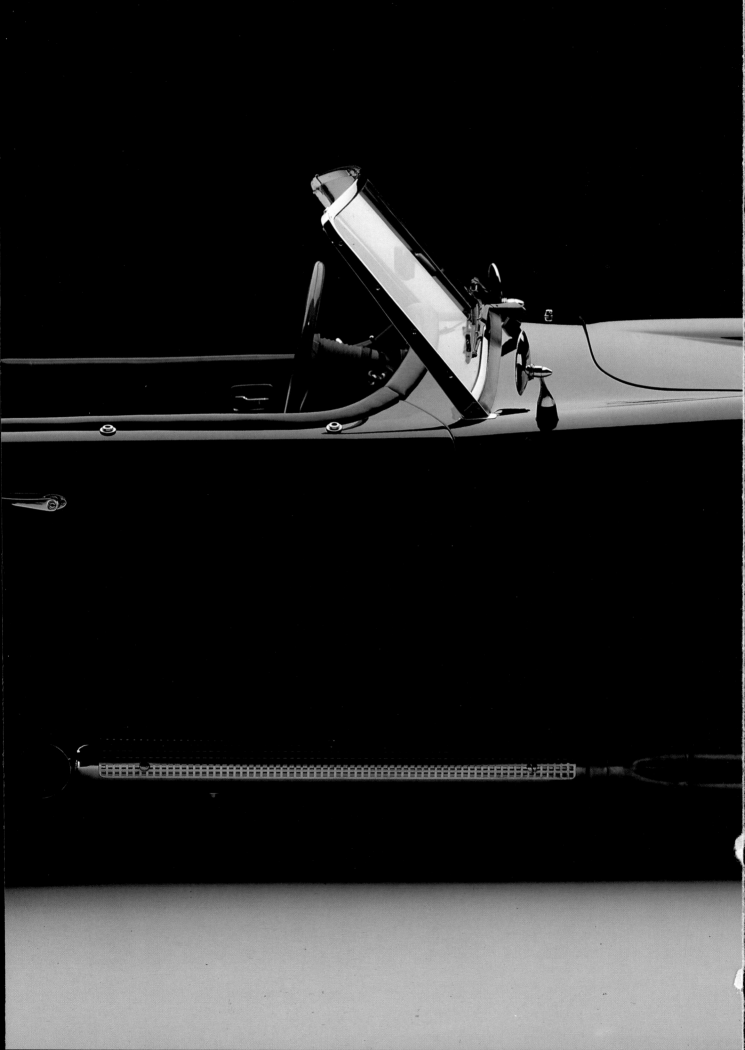

**Winner in 1952:
Mercedes
1953: Lancia
1954: Ferrari**

accompanied the race as a reporter in a fourth 300 SL that was intended to serve as a mobile spare-parts depot.

For the fastest American Indianopolis drivers such as Tony Bettenhausen or the subsequent world champion Phil Hill, the extremely dangerous and fast Carrera Panamericana was a unique opportunity to put one over the established stars. The race was run along the 1,923 mile (3,077 kilometer) Pan-American Highway from the northern to the southern border of Mexico. Drivers had to cope with straights up to 56 miles (90 kilometers) long, hot, damp tracks through the rain forest, and mountain stages at heights of up to 11,000 feet (3,400 meters). The road was closed only near the finish; otherwise it was open to allcomers, whether on wheels or on foot. The ambitious Mercedes drivers covered nearly 7,000 miles (11,000 kilometers) while practising in luxury 300 saloons.

Mercedes spared no expense or effort in their attempts to win the treacherous race - more than 1,950 miles (3130 kilometers) had to be covered in five full-day stages under conditions that would be considered wholly unreasonable today. The superbly equipped fleet of four tried and tested silver Mercedes 300 SLs from Untertürkheim was accompanied by two trucks and 35 technicians.

However, in the short period available for preparation, the

Between 1954 and 1955, Ferrari's most important weapon in the battle for the long-distance world championship was this 375 MM Berlinetta. Ouput: about 340 bhp at 7,000 rpm; winner of the Mille Miglia

They risked life and limb for victory in Mexico

Continental firm had been unable to make available special tyres. Moreover, the team had no previous experience of this gruelling race in a foreign country. Thus some of the tyres supplied had the deep Nürburgring tread designed for winding circuits; their use was to prove fateful. Karl Kling remembers the first moments of terror: "Tehuantepec was just coming into sight.... There.... What was that? A bang... the car suddenly began to jump around like crazy and then to slip sideways over the asphalt.... It could only be a tyre. Just keep calm, keep calm, I shouted to myself, and finally I managed to get the SL under control and bring it to a halt. I tore open the cockpit door and scrambled out as fast as I could. I soon discovered the problem: a rear tyre had burst. We opened the boot, grabbed hold of the jack and changed the wheel with the flat tyre just as quickly as we could... My God, what a nice little surprise if that sort of thing was happening already, more than 90 miles from our first tyre depot. We raced through Tehuantepec at high speed. We had ust got through the town when another rear tyre burst. This time it was the other one. Cursing, I stopped. We worked like crazy in the baking heat. Hans threw his crash helmet into the car. It was making him too hot. The

Mercedes racing chief Alfred Neubauer was in his element (ABOVE). *2,062 miles (3,300 kilometers) right across Central America: a race sticker worth keeping. The Panamericana adventure attracted the best racing drivers*

Not a sluggish American jalopy, but a 300 bhp Mercury with Troy Ruttman at the wheel

*Giovanni Bracco with his
prototype Ferrari 250 S
Berlinetta, Mercedes' strongest
rival in 1952*

*In 1952 in Mexico, crash-
barriers were seen as
luxuries. In the inevitable
pile-ups drivers and cars
became targets for
sensation-seeking
photographers. The
world's last race on open
roads had become too
dangerous: in 1954, the
Panamericana was
abandoned*

95

The Panamericana and Le Mans captured the interest of the public

tyre treads had too great a depth of rubber, apparently. The long straights did the rest. That was typical of the Mexican Carrera Panamericana, a race full of surprises."

This of course was just the beginning of an eventful journey: things were soon to get even worse. Kling goes on: "Then came that awful moment I won't forget in a hurry. The needle on the rev counter had swung up to 5,400 rpm. Since I was in fourth gear, that meant I was travelling at about 137 mph (220 kph)....

Suddenly I saw a black object hurtling towards me. There was a loud bang as if a hand grenade had gone off.... Splinters of windscreen were flying all over the place. A damned dangerous situation. I was struggling like crazy with the car, and needed the whole width of the road to get it back under control." A vulture had flown up in front of the car and crashed through the windscreen. Everybody in the maintenance depot was very agitated of course. Kling recalls how he reacted to the torrent of questions: "In reply I just flung the vulture down at their feet."

The extremely well-prepared Ferrari drivers led the race for two-thirds of the way. Four vehicles had been specially built in Maranello for the world-famous Carrera: the three 340 Mexico Berlinettas for Ascari, Villoresi and Chinetti and the 250 S Berlinetta for Bracco, who the same year had won the Mille Miglia from Karl Kling.

360,000 spectators at the Le Mans 24-hour race (FAR LEFT). The safety controls during races in the 40s and 50s (the picture above shows the 1958 Avus race in Berlin) protected neither spectators nor drivers. Car number 9 is the winner, a Porsche RSK

FAR LEFT: *the fast Veritas Meteor;* RIGHT, *red Porsche 356/2;* ABOVE: *James Dean with his Porsche Spyder*

However, Ferrari's plans did not work out. Ascari suffered bad luck right from the beginning and came off the road. Villoresi completed the Mexico City-Leon stage at the amazing average speed of 109.3 mph (175 kph), but then had to retire with transmission trouble. The talented daredevil Bracco also had to retire because of a mechanical fault, after he had held the overall lead for a long time. Only Chinetti remained among the leaders, but he was no match for the silver racers on the final stage, which was 231 miles (370 kilometers) of straight road.

Karl Kling and Hermann Lang took the lead here, having been hard on the heels of the Ferraris all the way, and won an impressive first victory in the New World for the improving Mercedes-Benz team.

The first three teams were:

1. Karl Kling and Hans Klenk

(Germany) in a Mercedes-Benz 300 SL; 18:51:19 hours; average speed 103.22 mph (165.153 kph)

2. Hermann Lang and Erwin Grupp (Germany) in a Mercedes-Benz 300 SL; 19:26:30 hours; average speed 100.07 mph (160.119 kph)

3. Luigi Chinetti and Jean Lucas

(Italy/USA) in a Ferrari 340 Mexico; 19:32:45 hours; average speed 99.54 mph (159.266 kph)

(Source: Günther Molter, former chief press officer at Daimler-Benz)

Stirling Moss and his legendary Mercedes 300 SLR. Winner of the sports-car world championship in 1955 as a result of victories in the Mille Miglia/Brescia-Rome, the Northern Ireland Tourist Trophy and the Targa Florio on Sicily

In 1955, Porsche sold the open-top 550 to private racing teams who won innumerable races in it, beating much more powerful front-engined sports cars

THE COURAGE TO EXPERIMENT WITH SPEED

David against Goliath. The lightweight Porsche 550s show their heavier rivals the way

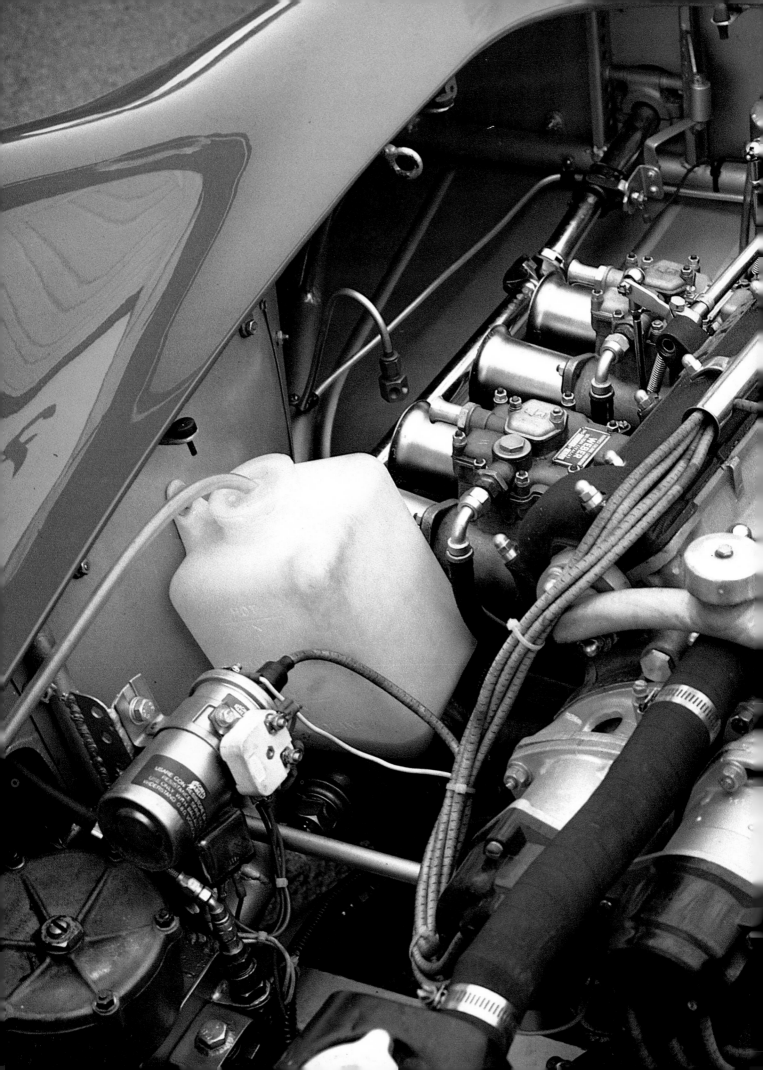

In 1957, the six-cylinder Maserati 300 S won the constructors' world championship. This massive 4-cylinder 450 S of 1958 was the last racing engine of the front-engined era. Ouput: 450 bhp

103

**Missed heartbeats:
trying to outbrake
one's rival at 185 mph**

The first automobile and motorcycle race in Germany after the war was the Karlsruhe Triangle Race. The racing circuit comprised what is now the Karlsruhe motorway intersection. A year after the end of the war, on 29 September 1946, 200 vehicles filled the paddock. More than 50,000 spectators lined the two and a quarter mile (3.4 kilometer) circuit, with its three hairpin bends. There were very few practice laps, since petrol was in short supply. The superior members of society drove to the race in their Opel Olympias with wood gas distillers. After a fairly vehement argument with the police about authorization, the first post-war 'German Grand Prix' got under way. Pre-war 328 BMWs took the first three places. To his own surprise, Karl Kling came second in the overall classification and was promptly engaged by former BMW designer Ernst Loof to race his new Veritas sports car in coming races.

The Veritas consisted of the BMW 328 power unit and a racy streamlined body. The number one works driver for the Veritas was Toni Ulmen. Because it was the first and therefore the oldest, his Veritas had been disrespectfully christened 'Grandmother' by the fans.

In Munich there was a sports car race round the Theresienwiese (the site of the famous beer festival). The barrier between the cars and the spectators consisted of 50 bales of straw at the start and finish line and a lot of large trees. At the race in Hamburg's

"Races are won on the brakes" - so said Stirling Moss after his victory in the 1955 Mille Miglia. The 1957 Lister Chevrolet, bearing the number 76, sits right down on the front springs when the brakes are applied

A 1959 Lister Jaguar at Laguna Secca (FAR LEFT). In the last few years of front-engined racing, the small English makers such as Elva, Marcos, Lister, Cooper and Lotus - described by Enzo Ferrari as do-it-yourself workshops - conquered the wealthy private racing team market. The "do-it-yourselfers" snatched many a victory away from Ferrari. LEFT: the famous SU carburetors of English sports cars

city park, 65,000 spectators lined the track with its pavé surface.

However, the German motor racing scene was soon to outgrow these modest post-war beginnings. Races with famous names were soon being held, but initially these were only in other European countries or overseas.

The famous endurance races of the 1950s were tremendously popular with the general public - the current enthusiasm for motor-racing is only modest in comparison. Radio commentators kept millions of listeners glued to their sets when the new Mercedes 300 SL entered the arena to compete against the powerful Italian Ferraris, Lancias and Maseratis, the British Aston Martins and Jaguars and the few French Gordinis in the Mille Miglia and the Le Mans 24-hour race. In 1952 Giovanni Bracco in his new 3-liter Ferrari 250 S Berlinetta beat the Mercedes works drivers in the Mille Miglia, but in the Le Mans race the six-cylinder light alloy-bodied Mercedes coupés driven by Hermann Lang and Fritz Riess notched up the first significant post-war German victory.

Alongside the British, Italian, German and French sports cars of the 1950s, many of them with large and powerful engines, there cavorted a less powerful but lighter and more agile car that pointed the way to the future: the rear-engined sports car designed by Professor Ferdinand Porsche. The very first pure Porsche design, the 356 prototype of 1948, built for the most

Jaguar D Types won the Le Mans 24-hour race from 1955 to 1957. The 16 examples of this model, fitted with 250 bhp engines, were real Porsche-killers. The monocoque chassis was made of riveted aluminium sheets. Its rivals were still using tubular framing

Porsche: a small pike in the carp pond

part out of parts from the VW Beetle, scored a sensational victory in the 1100cc class in the Le Mans 24-hour race. The subsequent Porsche 550s and 718s, introduced in 1953, were considered hot favourites for victory in their class on all types of racing, rally and mountain circuits. In the Targa Florio, however, Porsche were overall winners in 1956 and 1959.

When production of the type 356 finally ceased in 1965, more than 76,000 had been produced - exactly 75,500 more than Ferdinand Porsche had dared to predict in 1949. Since then, Porsche has become one of the most respected members of the world sports car elite.

The 1950s, however, were overshadowed by perhaps the most serious accident in racing history. It happened in 1955 at the Le Mans 24-hour race, when the Mercedes driver Pierre Levegh had a terrible crash in his 300 SLR: 82 spectators died with him. A short time after the accident, senior management in Stuttgart ordered the two remaining Mercedes cars, which were the favourites to win, to withdraw from the race.

American HMW 4.5 liter sports-racing car (FAR LEFT) with a Maserati engine. A really tough customer. The purely functional cockpit (LEFT) of a 1960 Ferrari. Shelby 7 liter Cobra, the 480 bhp powerhouse (BELOW)

Ferrari 250 TR with 2,953 cc Colombo engine, giving 230 bhp at 7,500 rpm. Bodywork by Scaglietti. A very rare car even at the time

109

Mid-engined sports cars, such as this very successful Cooper Maserati, won many races in 1963 against more powerful front-engined cars. Its better handling and lower weight produced faster lap times

THE EXPANSION OF ENDURANCE RACING

*The mid-engined sports racers of the
1970s gave private entrants no chance*

Carlos Page in the Ferrari 312 PB in the 1,000 kilometer race at Zeltweg, Austria. 3-liter, flat 12-cylinder engine, 450 bhp at 12,500 rpm

113

Porsche versus Ferrari - motor racing at its toughest

The great period of the world championships for so-called prototype sports cars in endurance races was between 1965 and 1971. More than 200,000 spectators made their way to the 1,000 kilometer race at the Nürburgring at the end of the 1960s. A further 50,000 fans were able to watch Germany's most important endurance race without paying. The 1969 Le Mans 24-hour race was watched by no fewer than 368,000 spectators.

The reason for this enthusiasm lay almost wholly in the fact that the teams were very evenly matched. It was a battle of the giants. The Ferrari type 512 S 5-liter sports car lined up against the 12-cylinder Porsche 917. The jokers in the pack were the Ford GT 40 from John Wyer's witches' kitchen and Jim Hall's sensational Chaparral. Its enormous rear wing and the three-speed automatic transmission for the 5-liter, V-8 Chevrolet fuel injection engine were of great technical interest. Finally, there was a pack of 3-liter prototypes from Alfa Romeo, Abarth, Chevron, Lotus, Matra, Porsche and Renault. There was no shortage of excitement.

During the 1971 1,000 kilometer race at Brands Hatch, the leaders Jo Siffert and Derek Bell in the quickest Porsche 917 lost the obligatory spare wheel as they drove out of the pits. Race control showed Derek Bell the black flag, which meant he had to make an immediate pit stop. Desperate attempts were made to find a suitable

The races between the 5-liter Porsche 917 and the Ferrari 512 P were battle of machines. FAR LEFT: *the red Ferrari team at Monza.* BELOW, *the duel on the Parabolica bend, fought out in the night*

Endurance racing at Grand Prix speeds

The Ferrari 275 LMs (BELOW) *were intended to win laurels as Gran Turismo cars. Drivers had to drive with total commitment to compete against the faster pure competition cars*

spare wheel. Finally, in six frantic minutes, the mechanics hammered out a wheel rim of the wrong size to fit the tiny storage space. The Porsche pair came second in the overall placings, behind Toine Hezemans and Rolf Stommelen in the Alfa Tipo 33.

In the 1971 Sebring 12-hour race Jo Siffert ran out of fuel. The Swiss driver borrowed a moped from a spectator and went to fetch some petrol from the pits. Siffert received a four-lap penalty for receiving unauthorized assistance, but still came fifth in the overall placings and gained a few world championship points.

The internal rivalry in John Wyer's Porsche team shows how hard, and also how recklessly, cars were driven in those days. In 1971, Jo Siffert and Pedro Rodriguez were in the lead at Watkins Glen. The two works drivers touched several times as they braked for a corner. Finally, as Siffert tried again to overtake, the Mexican swung right out, forcing Siffert to the edge of the track, where I was standing, taking close-up photographs of the two works cars. A sideways leap worthy of an Olympic athlete saved me from serious injury, but my camera equipment had had it. Siffert and Rodriguez were shaken up by the collision and headed for the pits to check their damaged cars (which were after all capable of over 200 mph or 320 kph). The Alfa pair of Andrea de Adamich and Henry Pescarolo ended up winners, much to their amusement.

More racing drivers died in the years between 1967 and 1972 than at

An air-cooled Porsche 917 12-cylinder (ABOVE) - the most powerful 5 liter engine, 650 bhp. (RIGHT) the Chaparral Chevrolet, the first rear winged car, which won the 1,000 km Nürburgring race

Power gone wild: too little safety, too much risk

any time before or after. At the 1967 Monaco Grand Prix, Lorenzo Bandini met his death because of a driving error. The two Lotus works drivers, Jim Clark and Mike Spence, died in 1968 at Hockenheim and Indianapolis respectively. In the same year, the Ferrari drivers Ignazio Giunti and Luigi Scarfiotti suffered fatal injuries in sports car races. The unprecedented career of Jochen Rindt ended tragically in 1970 when he crashed into the barriers at Monza. Pedro Rodriguez burnt to death in the Noris race in the summer of 1971. Just three months later, his rival Jo Siffert had an accident at Brands Hatch as a result of a suspension fault. Finally, the fatal accident suffered by the Lola works driver Joakim Bonnier in the 1972 Le Mans 24-hour race showed that the safety of vehicles and race tracks required thorough reconsideration.

Eventually, at the end of 1972, the racing authorities in Paris banned 5-liter racers from taking part in the endurance world championship.

The Porsche 2.2-liter long-tailed prototypes won Le Mans from Ford GT 40s and Ferrari sports cars with twice the power. With a top speed of 228 mph (365 kph), the white six-cylinder cars were miracles of aerodynamics. Gerhard Mitter leads Kurt Ahrens

The Ferrari 250/275 LMs were developed in 1963 as GT cars. The 2,953cc V-12 mid-mounted engine was increased to 3.3 liters and 320 bhp

119

CAN-AM RACERS: THE ACES OF THE CIRCUITS

The most powerful of the big bangers could put 1100 bhp onto the road

The quickest and most powerful circuit racing cars in the mid-1970s were the CanAm racing cars. Jackie Oliver's UOP Shadow DN 2 at Riverside in 1973

Big money for short races. Hourly wage: 40,000 dollars

Most CanAm races were run over two legs. Maximum race distance: 225 miles (360 kilometers). RIGHT: *the 5-liter Zipper Alfa*

For ten years, from 1965 to 1975, North Americans in both Canada and the USA were able to witness a series of sports car races that were quite unique in both sporting and technical terms. Known officially as the Canadian American Challenge Cup, the CanAm races dispensed with all restrictions on engine size and weight. Open and closed cars could line up together on the starting line. The drivers earned a great deal more money here than in the endurance world championship in Europe.

In 1969, the minimum weight for cars in the 5-liter racing class was 1,760 lbs. The drivers of the quickest cars had at least 820 bhp at their command. There was seldom much mechanical damage because the races were run over a distance of 225 miles at most.

In the 1960s, the McLarens, with Bruce McLaren and Dennis Hulme at the wheel, scored the greatest number of victories. Porsche's first appearance at Watkins Glen in 1969 was a failure. Jo Siffert, driving the obviously underpowered 3-liter 908/3 sports car, with an output of 365 bhp, was left trailing.

In the 1970 season, the Porsche 917 started on its all-conquering career. In just a few years, it won innumerable victories; it was this car, more than any other Porsche, that established the marque's reputation as a technological pacesetter for years to come.

World champion Dennis Hulme - CanAm millionaire

Mark Donohue

World star
Jackie Stewart

François Cevert, the fastest Lola driver

CanAm luminary:
Jo Bonnier

V8 production engines from the USA are robust and relatively cheap.

The cost-benefit ratio of the CanAm racing cars is ideal. LARGE PICTURE: *McLaren M 20;* SMALL PICTURE: *Porsche 917/30 with George Follmer*

After victories in the 1970 and 1971 Constructors' World Championships, Porsche put its involvement in the European motor racing scene temporarily on the back burner in order to concentrate on the CanAm championships, which were extremely effective for publicity purposes. The success story continued. In 1972, Porsche won the CanAm series. In 1973, with the legendary Mark Donohue at the wheel, this success was repeated on an even more triumphal scale; he notched up seven individual wins, which put Porsche way ahead of the rest of the field as overall winner of the CanAm series.

The victorious car in 1972 was a Porsche 917/10 with turbocharger, a 5-liter, 12-cylinder engine giving 1,000 bhp, and weighing 1,716 lb (780 kilograms) (excluding fuel). That for 1973 was a Porsche 917/30 with turbocharger, 1,100 bhp and a weight of 1,804 lb (820 kilograms) (excluding fuel). The 917/30 racers are by far the most powerful cars ever to have been driven on a race track.

Donohue lapped a closed circuit in this car at the then unbelievable speed of 222.4 mph (355.86 kph), which was to remain the record lap speed until 1979, when a Mercedes clocked 251.25 mph (402.00 kph) at Nardo in Italy.

A "wheelstander", a type of funny dragster. The driver looks through transparent floor panels and steers the car by differential braking on each rear wheel

FUNNY CARS REACH
280 MPH (450 KPH)

The fastest accelerators are the
2,500 bhp dragsters

Only funny dragsters can get up to 303 mph (486 kph) in 5.3 seconds.

With infernal noise and smoking tyres, the daredevil dragsters hurtle from the start, watched in the USA by some 4 million people every year

It is well known in European racing circles that good money can be earned from motor sport in America. The winner of the Indianopolis 500 receives a million dollars. In order to earn a similar sum a Formula 1 racing driver would have to win about ten Grand Prix races - and the risks are far greater. The handful of successful dragster drivers pocket even greater sums in prize money. At the two most important events of the season, the winter and summer nationals, the winner is rewarded with prize money worth about $1.6 million dollars. Nowhere else on earth can so much money be earned in 5.3 seconds.

Funny car dragsters can accelerate more quickly than any other type of car. With their 2,600 bhp engines, the supercharged sprinters fight it out with each other in single combat. The best

drivers cover the quarter mile (402 meter) straight in 5.3 seconds. By the time they reach the finishing line, they might be travelling at 300 mph (486 kph). By way of comparison, one of the fastest recent production sports cars, the Ferrari F 40, accelerates to 125 mph (200 kph) in 12 seconds.

The regulations require that the cars have 75% of the original bodywork of a production car. The side profile must

Looking like some lone warrior, the dragster driver waits for the start, thickly trussed in fireproof overalls

The green light gives the signal for the start. The slicks are completely distorted by the strain of 2,500 bhp tugging on the rear wheels (MAIN PICTURE). Successful funny car teams have an annual budget of $10 million

"It takes money to make money" - racing drivers' saying.

No victories without money. Even the American Army sponsors funny dragster teams (LEFT)

be 90% identical to the original measurements. Very special technology is concealed in the floor of the car. Thanks to the concave shaping of the floorpan, down pressure rises continuously. As a result, the cars sink to a distance of about 2 inches (5 centimeters) from the ground. The high down pressure reduces wheelspin on the 20 inch (50 centimeter) wide tyres.

When second gear is engaged, by means of an electromagnetic device, the driven wheels spin again, even at 130 mph (210 kph). This is a very dangerous moment, since at the same moment the 2,600 bhp, 8-cylinder engine rises in its very flexible mountings, shifting the weight to one side. During this interval of a fraction of a second, the driver has to correct the car's slight deviation with the steering. A split second later, the car is travelling at 250 mph (400 kph), and driving in a straight line becomes a real problem. For dragster fans, the most spectacular funny cars are the pinnacle of motor sport. There is something in motor racing to suit every taste.

MOTOR SPORT AS PUBLICITY

Production sports cars no longer bring in the money on the race track

Today's Group C racing cars can no
longer be compared from a technical
viewpoint with production sports cars;
here a Mazda GTO

Too few spectators at sports car races

The sports car world championship is no box-office hit. The public wants to see works teams competing

Formula 1 is still the long-running success story of motor sport. This is where the best racing drivers are to be found, and racing politics are extremely lively. The power of the sponsors is a critical factor in victory or defeat - sometimes even the smaller teams get a look-in, if they can throw better, more expensive machinery into the battle. Excitement, sport and show business - is it enough to satisfy all those involved? The situation in sports car racing is quite different. Second-class drivers often contest third-class races in first-class cars. Only a bare handful of cars have any chance of victory. The prize money bears no relationship to the risk, as the fatal accidents testify. Even the participation of more manufacturers in recent years, such as Mercedes-Benz through the Sauber team, as well as Peugeot and some Japanese firms, has not made the sports car championship a box office success.

Spectators want to see official works teams from Ford, Jaguar, Mercedes and Porsche competing, but so far their hopes have been dashed. If BMW, Lancia and Renault were also to join in the fray, the Japanese might begin to take a more serious interest.

Spectators and advertising men alike enthused over the 800 bhp Sauber Mercedes, top speed of 240 mph (385 kph). Are Daimler-Benz making a comeback?

Arbitrary regulations restrict rallying

The 600 bhp Audi Quattro Rallye was a victim of the senselessly autocratic policy on regulations pursued by the international motor sport commission in Paris

Like the fast Audi Quattros, the new Peugeot 405 T16 four-wheel drive rally cars were excluded from the rally world championship

Spectators should recognize the cars they see in rallies. The Peugeot 405 T16 is a wolf in standard sheep's clothing hiding racing internals: 500 bhp mid-mounted engine, variable 4-wheel drive and height adjustment to suit the stage. Top speed about 160 mph (260 kph)

Successful racing drivers have to be cool and calculating, both in ensuring the safety of their equipment and in calculating their fees. Indianapolis millionaire Rick Mears (FAR RIGHT). Next to him, sports car veteran and world champion Derek Bell

Newcomer Lada: Motor racing in Russia

Virtually unnoticed in Central Europe, Russian rally and racing cars are developing into interesting competition vehicles. FAR LEFT, *the latest Lada, and to its right the Vostok racing car, similar to West European Formula 3 cars*

Most motor sport experts know very little about motor sport in the former Soviet Union. In fact, in the very early days of Grand Prix racing, the Russian A. Soldatenkov met with some success, for example in the French Grand Prix. A Russo-Balt touring car once won the Monte Carlo Rally, defeating established teams entered by the likes of Peugeot, Fiat and Mercedes. With the exception of Formula 1 and Group C races, motor sport is now pursued very actively in Eastern Europe. Estonija racing cars, similar to our Formula 3 racers, are built at the KFZ plant in Tallin: power output is about 160 bhp. The most interesting rally car from the technical point of view is the new Lada 2105-WTFS, with its 160 bhp engine and a top speed of 120 mph (192 kph). The Lada is homologated as a Group B car.

Rallycross races for heavy trucks are spectacular events. The Russians scored their greatest success in the punishing Paris-Dakar rally, when in 1988 the decisive overall winner in the heavy truck class was a Soviet LIAZ.

HIGH-TECH WOLVES IN OLD CLOTHES

An original 1934 Ford coupé made do with 65 bhp; today's street rod has 450

The shape is 50 years old, but under the non-existent hood is a gleaming 450 bhp Ford V8 supercharged engine. Street rods are new, slightly crazy sports cars in old clothes

143

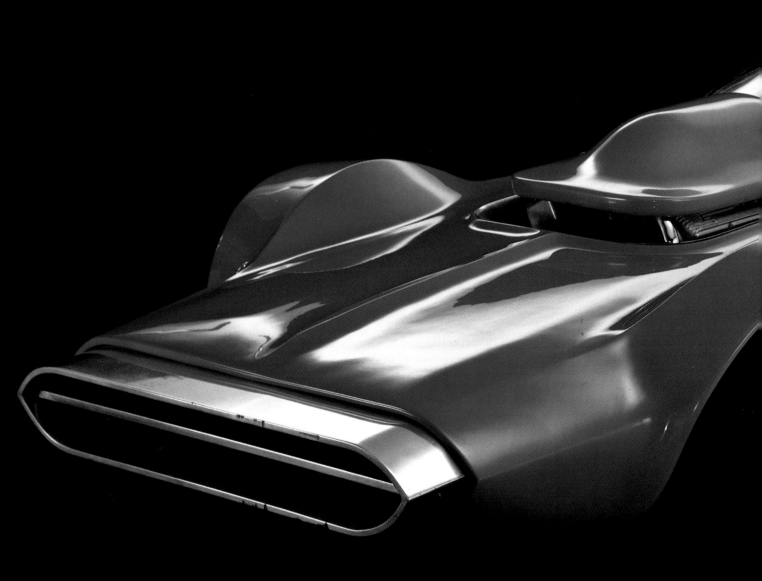

This home-made street rod was christened "Star Trek". The taste may be questionable, but there can be no dispute about its performance: Chevrolet V8 supercharged engine on a CanAm racing car chassis

Street rods: Cars to make you laugh or cry

Exuberant shapes, futuristic designs - these are the home-made street rods from California. Their sporting character is beyond doubt

Modern production cars are virtually perfect machines. Soulless things, created in wind tunnels, shaped by marketing men who count every penny. Many Americans and not a few Europeans are quite deliberately shunning the luxurious offerings that roll off the production line and are building their own cars, known as street rods.

These provocatively glittering blunderbusses appear completely untouched by technical progress. The older or more crazy the bodywork, the better. When a street rod in the guise of a 50-year old Ford, but powered by a 350 bhp engine, beats the latest Chevrolet Stingray from one traffic light to the next by a distance of five lengths, many sports car enthusiasts are absolutely horrified. However, a modern sports car corners more quickly of course.

A 500 bhp Ford Coupé (ABOVE). Flame designs are popular for Mercury Lowriders

A fast home-made three-wheeler, with a 120 bhp engine. A cross between sports car and motor-cycle, top speed 125 mph (200 kph)

The Mercedes 4-rotor Wankel-engined sports car reached 187.5 mph (300 kph) in 1970. At 350 bhp, the C 111 epitomizes the racy, high-powered sports car. The aerodynamically perfect body shape is thanks to the wind tunnel

GERMAN FLIERS

*Felix Wankel's rotary piston engine was
the sensation of the 1970s*

Until 1988, this Mercedes C 111-IV held the absolute world record for a closed circuit with a speed of 252.486 mph (403.978 kph). Experimental engineer Dr Hans Liebold set the record on the test track at Nardo, Southern Italy

The C 111 broke CanAm winner Mark Donohue's record, set in the 1,100 bhp Porsche 917/30. at a record speed of 222.408 mph (355.854 kph) in 1975. Here is a preliminary design for the legendary C 111 IV produced for wind tunnel tests but already fitted with the 5-liter V8 engine with twin turbochargers

TVR 420: 300 bhp, 0 to 60 mph in under 5 seconds.

Aston Martin V8. Traditional handcrafting.

British open car enthusiasts take their weather as it comes

The silver Ronart W 152 is the latest English roadster in the style of the 1950s (MAIN PICTURE). *The mechanics are from the Jaguar XJ6 or XJ12; max. 150 mph (240 kph)*

Britain has always been a particularly happy hunting ground for exotic sports cars, although today there is strong competition from elsewhere, even from Germany, where there is always a good market for new, exclusive sports cars. The Mercedes 8-cylinder engines are very popular as a basis for German exotica - the torquey 5.6-liter engine produces a solid 300 bhp, with only a little tuning. The 380 bhp AMG engines are more reliable than many production power units with comparable performance.

Lorenz & Rankl of Tölz use Mercedes parts as the basis for their beautiful roadster, the Silver Falcon. The style of the 1950s is still alive here. Even more nostalgic is the Elisar, produced by GFG in Gronau. With styling borrowed from the Mercedes 540K, this high-quality sports car has found its niche in the market, particularly in America, alongside such established favourites as the British Panther Kallista.

Unlike certain of the smaller British manufacturers, German sports car companies make both the chassis and the bodywork in-house. Kit cars are frowned upon in Germany. In the light of the high performance of some of these cars, which are capable of between 140 and 175 mph (230 to 280 kph), the German authorities would not

Fine racers from Germany. Dream cars with safety

The Lotus Super Seven (MAIN PICTURE) *supplied by Caterham with virtually any level of performance. The model for the successful small-production sports car for 20 years*

The Isdera Imperator 108i: 175 mph (280 kph), Mercedes V8 engine

give any kit cars type approval. German small production sports cars are not cheap. The price for a top speed of 156 mph (250 kph) and a power output of 300 bhp is around $94,000.

Virtually no other vehicle has enthralled sports car enthusiasts more over the years than the AC Cobra, with brute power from its various big American engines and sure-footed handling from its tubular backbone chassis. The Cobra's basic design is 30 years old and was developed in Britain, at the instigation of the American driver Carroll Shelby, as a much more powerful variant of the 2-liter AC Ace. Various independent companies have produced Cobra replicas since production of the original ceased, many, such as the recent German version called the Stallion (see pages 88 to 90), with improvements such as a a more rigid tubular frame and a semi-trailing arm rear axle. But now there is no need to buy a replica, as AC Cars have themselves produced a beautifully made new Cobra, which in spite of emission control gets 345 bhp from its 5.0 liter Ford V8 and combines remarkable docility with a staggering 0-62 mph (0-100 kph) in 4.35 seconds. The price is about $120,000.

Silver Falcon by Lorenz & Rantel

GFG Elisar: quality in the style of the 540K

The view of the F 40 enjoyed by all other drivers, even the 200 owners of the Porsche 959

FERRARI F 40 - THE WORLD CHAMPION

The supreme machine from Maranello: the fastest, most powerful and most beautiful car in the world

Sporting supercars come equipped with the finest interiors. This is the stereo system in the Gemballa Porsche costing nearly $19,000

The name alone is a memorial: F stands for Ferrari and 40 for the 40 years' success. With 478 bhp and top speed of 202.5 mph (324 kph), Formula 1 technology has been transferred to series production

Timeless Elegance Pininfarina Design

Ferrari bodywork sets the world standard. The 4-seater Mondial 8 (ABOVE); top speed 138 mph (221 kph). The Testarossa can reach 180 mph (290 kph)

Enzo Ferrari recalled: "If I had followed my wife's advice, I would have been working for the streetcar company, because she considered this a good job, and one that promised security. But I always felt attracted to fast cars." And it was just as well he did. Enzo Ferrari's sports cars are unique creations. Unmistakable in their charisma and uncompromising in their brilliant technical specification, they are sports cars through and through: performance on the road comes before comfort.

With the creation of the F 40, which he left behind as a sort of legacy after his sudden death in the middle of August 1988, the self-willed commendatore once again proved himself

capable of forcing through this own ideas. The 3-liter eight-cylinder twin-turbocharged engine produces 478 bhp at 7,000 rpm and 1.1 bar boost pressure, powering the car to a top speed of 202.5 mph (324 kph). The Modena factory quotes a maximum engine speed of 7,750 rpm. Those acquainted with the free-revving

Ferrari engines will be able to imagine the potential of a racing version of the F 40 with 590 bhp and a top speed of some 237.5 mph (380 kph).

The rules governing international sports car racing do not yet permit the Ferrari F 40 to be entered for races, but this car has all the requirements for a successful racing career, while

stealing the show in any gathering of roadgoing sports cars.

The F 40 is fitted with the extremely successful electronic fuel injection system used in Ferrari Formula 1 racing cars.

RARITIES WITH EYE APPEAL

Many sports cars have that certain something. Charisma is often more important than sheer performance

55 mph (85 kph) speed-limit in America, but the Vector's 425 bhp V8 twin turbo-charger engine has a top speed of 234 mph. An exotic rarity

Developed for production-car racing, the BMW M1 today is an expensive and sought-after classic, with Giugiaro coachwork; standard version 277 bhp, racing version 470 bhp, Group C version 850 bhp

Lamborghini LP 400 S Countac, designed by a pupil of Bertone, combines sophisticated engineering with breath-taking styling. 375 bhp V12 engine; top speed: 193 mph (310 kph)

The De Tomaso Pantera is built to order in Modena. Output varies between 190 and 270 bhp. This shark-like 350 S, with a 5,763 cc, V8 engine and a top speed of 175 mph (280 kph), comes from the German car tuner Suhe

Both the very latest as well as the older sports cars of Italian origin prove that Italian bodywork designers really understand their craft. A successful shape endures. The Ferrari 250 GTO, now almost 30 years old, has such a special allure that connoisseurs today recognize it as a work of art. During the development of the new Ferrari F 40, Pininfarina put forward the almost old-fashioned view that "we must get the shape right first, and then the wind tunnel becomes useful for optimizing details". Ferrari's new masterpiece turned out to have correspondingly sweeping lines. The northern Italians are also keeping up a tradition of road performance that would be unimagin-

The Lancia Stratos (FAR LEFT) *won the world rally championship several times. Almost exact replicas are now being built in the USA. The new BMW Z1 roadster* (LEFT) *is a courageous attempt to compete against the established sports car makers using large-scale production technology*

able even at Porsche: "The Ferrari F 40 is a racing car for the open road. As light, rigid and quick as possible." Expressed in figures, the F 40 weighs a very considerable 1,025 lbs (466 kilograms) less than the Porsche 959. Considerable use is made of the more rigid Kevlar in place of aluminium. The complete door, together with its plastic

window, weighs just 7.5 lb (3.4 kilograms). The padding on the Kevlar bucket seat is less than a quarter of an inch (4 millimeters) thick - even the seats in the Group C Porsche 962 are more comfortable. Supersports cars with even higher performance are on the way from Italy. There will soon be a new Lamborghini with a 500 bhp

engine, and since 1987 Ferrari have been subjecting a 650 bhp engine to long-term tests in the GTO Evoluzione.

The president of Ferrari, Signor Razelli, declares: "The most powerful sports car on the market must always be a Ferrari."

It seems that no one can escape the fascination of a beautiful shape. The

171

America's famous ever-green, Chevrolet Corvette gives high performance at low engine speeds and from a large displacement engine. The Callaway twin turbo gives 365 bhp at just 2,750 rpm

The technically refined four-wheel drive Porsche 959 offers slightly less performance than the F 40 - 450 bhp, top speed 197 mph (315 kph). Produced in a limited edition of 200

Compared to the F 40, the Porsche 959 is a sheep in wolf's clothing that can be driven uncomplainingly in stop-go urban traffic. This masterpiece is already regarded as a milestone in automobile history

A video camera as a rear-view mirror? For the clients, this $18,500 extra is as important as body work changes of the Porsche 928 S4 Mark II (MAIN PICTURE)

The Gemballa Cyrrus, based on the Porsche 930 Turbo, is a customizer's masterpiece but costs about twice the standard model

Mercedes 540K from the 1930s has a timeless elegance, and will still be attracting new admirers in the year 2000.

Like other classics of the modern era, the evergreen Porsche 911, now 30 years old, is visually fairly plain in its basic form. The company has never believed in making purely cosmetic changes - much to the delight of all

Porsche enthusiasts. The car customizers exploit this situation to their own advantage, proving emphatically that visual and technical improvements can be made - but at a price.

Purchasers of the Gemballa Avalanche 911 Coupé produced in Leonberg (see last double page) have to pay around three times the price of the standard product. The aerodynamics (cd value) are better than that of the standard models, due to the addition at the front of an electronically adjustable front spoiler

Car customizers: the best are imaginative, fully-fledged designers

Plastic bolt-on goodies is not enough. Customers want an outstanding vehicle and not one seen everywhere. This Cyrrus costs about $155,000

and the optimization of the rear end. The chassis is fitted with additional struts, stabilizers and the best shock absorbers, normally used only for racing. A mere facelift would benefit neither customers nor the company's reputation if the car's stability were worse than that of standard models.

Gemballa's leather-upholstered interiors are considered the best available, and each customer gets an individually designed interior. This requires good ideas and costs a great deal of money and time, but the expense is worthwhile. BMW subcontracts work to these specialists in Leonberg, where prototypes commissioned by firms from around the world are built in a department which is hermetically sealed off from the outside world.

Gemballa was recognized as an international automobile manufacturer in 1985. Today, the company employs 60 people. Porsche and Lotus also developed out of very small workshops run by enthusiasts. Clearly good ideas and professional competence can still provide the foundation for a career in the automobile industry in Germany.

Nobody can predict today whether there will still be 220 mph (350 kph) sports cars in the year 2000. Car

Sports car 2000: superfast, aerodynamic, driver-friendly

A look into the future: the Chevrolet Indianapolis experimental car. The American automobile giants still see highly sophisticated sports cars as ideal for publicity

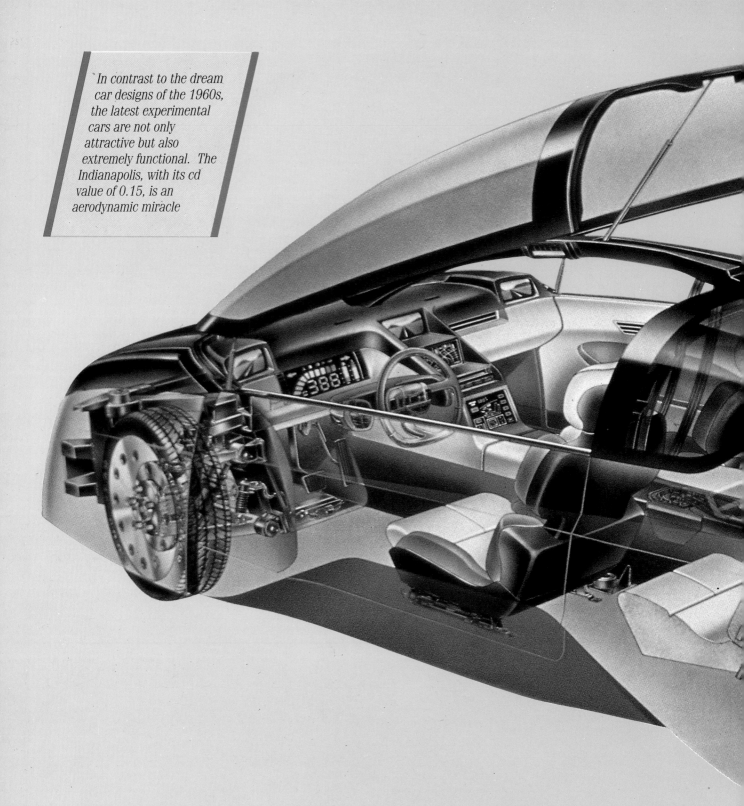

In contrast to the dream car designs of the 1960s, the latest experimental cars are not only attractive but also extremely functional. The Indianapolis, with its cd value of 0.15, is an aerodynamic miracle

designers take a pragmatic view of the future, considering that the car of the year 2000 will look much the same as today's better proportioned cars.

Forward thinkers see a need for improving interior design and aerodynamics. Very few sports cars have driver-friendly interiors. The seats are either too hard or too soft, and what may look smart is usually inadequately tailored to suit individual body sizes. No discriminating racing or rally driver would be satisfied with such cars.

Most sports cars also make unreasonable demands on drivers; the steering for a start requires the strength of an ox at parking speeds. Then the restricted view of the road from the low driving position can be a real problem. Awkward gear-changing, heavy clutches and fierce brakes - only he-men with bulging arm and leg muscles can take pleasure in driving

Fuel scarcity will return to the agenda sooner or later. General Motors developed this superfast Sunraycer - in 1988 it won the 1,875 mile (3,000 kilometer) Australian Solar Rally with a top speed of 70.6 mph (113 kph)

such cars.

The scope for improving automobile aerodynamics is still far from being exhausted. Few standard sports cars have a ground-effect floor, which is desirable if bends are to be taken really fast. The airstream gets blocked in the wheel housings, although elastic wheel covers which would make a sports car safer and quicker are now technically feasible. And a variable front profile would considerably improve the handling of such cars, even when travelling in a straight line.

Who will be making the most beautiful sports cars in the year 2000?

Gas turbines and Wankel engines are in fashion again in America

General Motors recently amazed the industry with a new gas turbine-powered experimental car. The Chevrolet Express (both photographs) is silky-smooth and has better acceleration than cars powered by standard petrol engines

Experts see the Californian design centre operated jointly by Japanese and American companies as the source of the most creative ideas, from which the decisive impetus will emerge.

One question is asked repeatedly: will the small sports car manufacturers survive? It has been shown in the past that the market for really exclusive sports cars is no less profitable in economically difficult times than in others. Supersports cars will certainly not become extinct, but drivers and customers will surely exert greater pressure on manufacturers than they do today. By the year 2000, the right to have a say in the technical design and equipment of sports cars will be taken for granted by increasingly demanding customers.

Index
Page numbers in brackets
indicate illustrations

Acknowledgments

Transedition Books would like to thank the following: Günther Molter; Bodo Fischer; Jürgen Riesterers; Ferrari importing agents, Autoexpo of Stuttgart; Michael Rau; Charles Proche.
Audi AG/H. Dieter, L. Scharnagl: pp136-137; Aston Martin Lagonda Ltd, Newport Pagnell: p152, p153 (top), pp154-155; Autoexpo-Ferrari, Stuttgart: pp156-160; Autopress-Neckarsulm: pp74-75; Caterham, England: pp154-155 (bottom); Daimler-Benz AG, historisches Archiv, Stuttgart: pp2-5, pp22-25, pp42-43, pp58-6, pp84-85, pp134-135, pp148-149, pp150-151, back cover; Fiat, Heilbronn: p75 (bottom); Ford AG, Cologne: pp77 (bottom), p. 81; Pressebro Forster: pp170-171; Gemballa Automobile, Leonberg: pp8-9, p161, pp178-185, pp192-193; General Motors AG/Opel AG: p24 (bottom), p62 (top), pp78-79, pp80-83, pp172-173; GFG Gerhard Feldevert & Co, Gronau: pp154-155 (top right), pp184-189; Indianapolis Raceway Ltd: p25 (bottom), p25 (top); Isdera Automobile, Leonberg: p154 (left); L & M Motorshow Philip Morris GmbH: pp142-147; Lynx Cars, St Leonards on Sea: pp152-153 (bottom), p153 (top); Günther Molter, Gerlingen: pp94-95; Peugeot Deutschland: p137 (top), pp138-139; Porsche AG, Stuttgart: pp174-175, pp176-177; Renault Deutschland: p78 (top); Ronart Cars, Peterborough: pp152-153; Rothändle Raritäten Show: pp10-11, pp16-17, pp44-45, pp49-50; Stallion-Schmidt Motorsport, Nuremberg: pp88-89; "Sowjetunion heute", Cologne: pages pp140-141 (top); TVR Cars, Blackpool: pp152-153 (top left); ZEFA picture agency, Boschung, Düsseldorf: pp168-169. All other photographs: Hans G. Isenberg and Charles Proche. Jacket picture: National Motor Museum, Beaulieu, England. Design: Herbert Emmer, Asamwald/Stuttgart, and Wolfgang Kelling, Stuttgart.

German language text and photographs:
© Falken Verlag GmbH, 1991
English language edition © Transedition Books 1993
All rights reserved.
Translation: Andrew Wilson in association with First Edition Translations Ltd, Cambridge.

Printed in Slovenia.

Published in Germany in 1989 by Falken Verlag GmbH, Niedernhausen/Ts.
This edition published in the USA in 1993 by Chartwell Books, Inc., a Division of Book Sales, Inc., 110 Enterprise Avenue, Secaucus, New Jersey 07094.

ISBN 1 55521 934 9